Southern Goodness

CELESTIA
MOBLEY

READER NOTES:
All spoon measurements are level either teaspoon 5 ml, and tablespoons are assumed to be 15 ml. Unless otherwise stated, milk is assumed to be full fat (whole milk).

Times are given as a guide only. Preparation times differ according to techniques used by different people and cooking times may also vary from those given.

Those who have nut allergies should take notice that some of these recipes in this book contain nuts. Vegetarians should be aware that some of the ready-made ingredients within the recipes in this book may contain animal products. Always check the packaging before use.

To Kim Benton President of ABC Book Publishers, Inc.
Thanks for all your help and treating this book as if it was your own,
you went above and beyond to make Southern Goodness special.

9456 Ford Road
Bryceville, Florida 32009
southerngoodness.cooking
chefcelestia.com

ISBN: 978-0-9963671-0-3

Produced by
ABC Book Publishers, Inc.

Photography by
CJ and Marcia Nurse, BrandX Media
and
Jeff Westcott Photography

Book Design by
Jeanine Colombi-Quinn

Southern Goodness

CELESTIA
MOBLEY

Published by
Executive Chef Celestia Mobley, LLC.

Acknowledgements

I would like to first give thanks to my Lord and Savior Jesus Christ. If it were not for the Lord on my side where would I be? Really. I would like to thank and honor my best friend, my boyfriend, my lover, and my biggest supporter, my husband Varon Mobley. I love you even more now after 24 years of marriage. He always reminds me that he told me that, "My gift will make room for me" and boy was he right.

I'd like to thank my daughter Jasmine who taught me the meaning of unconditional love. There is no love like the love a mother has for a child. She is so kind, talented, beautiful, and smart. She gets it from me. Smile.

I would like to thank my baby sister, Lashawn Chieves; I can't imagine my life without her. Every life memory I have she was there. She has been one of my biggest cheerleaders and taste testers. I love her to the moon and back...Kissababy!!!

I would like to give a special thank you to my sister/friend Regina Thornton who helped me tremendously with her gift of words. I miss our all-nighters; they were always so much fun. You are amazing; this book would not be possible if you did not agree to help me. You really need to write a book in titled, "The Book of Gina." I love you, girl.

To my bishop, Vaughn McLaughlin, thank you, thank you, and thank you!!! For seeing the potential in me, and allowing me to use the Bistro as a platform to showcase my gifts. You are such a generous, kind, and loving man. I love you...that's my Bishop!

To my lady, Narlene McLaughlin, I cannot say enough about you. You have been my mentor, my friend, my counselor, my boss lady, my spiritual mother. I know you love me, and that you pray for me, and I appreciate that more than anything. You are my lady, I will love, and honor you always.

To my longtime best friends Sonya Armstrong, Ursula Jackson Brown, and Yelonda Whetstone Harvey, I love you guys to pieces our friendship of over 35 years has been amazing. We have shared so many great times together. When I need to talk, cry, or laugh you ladies have always been there for me. "Senior girls" will have a different meaning in a couple of years. Lord, we are getting old. Smile.

To my mother-in-law Annette Mobley you are so special to me. Thank you for being a part of my life. Thank you for loving me like the daughter you never had. You are small in stature, but you are huge with passion for your family. I love you, Ms. Annette...can you clean the chittlins this year? Smile.

To all my family, we are beyond blessed. Our elders left us with so much love, and spiritual knowledge. I love all of you, there is nothing like family, and my prayer is that we all have the love of Christ in our hearts. God bless you all!

Your humble servant,
Chef Celestia Mobley, CEC

Inspiration

Gloria Jean Williams

My mother, Gloria Jean Williams, is my rock and my inspiration. I am the woman I am today because of her. She loves the Lord, and walks in that love daily. She has such a kind spirit; she has never met a stranger. I inherited my gift of hard work, love for people, and servitude from her. She worked extremely hard, normally working from sun up to sundown. I was a latch-key kid, and many times had to make dinner for my sister and myself. I was only around the age of 8 or of course it was simple things that mostly went in the oven, however, I felt like such a big girl and loved every minute of it. I always say her culinary contribution to me was her love for entertaining. She was always having crab boils, fish frys, and barbecues. During the Holidays my sister and I still insist that she makes her famous oyster dressing – it is absolutely divine! She is such a wonderful cook. Her sacrifices and dedication to me and my sister will never be forgotten. I will always love and honor my beautiful Mother. MY ROCK!

Introduction

Jasmine Mobley

I'll start by saying this: Not too many kids can say they have a chef as a mom. That's right–my own personal Chef. Jealous? Smile. Dinner at my house was the equivalent to eating at a 5-star restaurant in my eyes. My dad and I ate very good, and although I wish I could've kept my mom's talent "hidden" (that way I could've kept her all to myself), in hind sight, it makes sense that there's no way that a gift like hers could be hidden.

Holidays were the best, there were only three people in our household, so understandably, we enjoyed having a lot of people over during special occasions. Hosting celebrations and bringing family together seemed natural and effortless for my mom. She made enough food to feed an army and always sent friends and family home with goodies from the oven.

To me, that's what Southern food and *Southern Goodness* is all about — *food for the soul* — it lifts your spirit and warms your heart. When it is made with love, it doesn't have to be fancy or complicated. My Mom's great food brought us to the table where we build upon the strong connections of family traditions. And that's the Celestia Mobley Way. I love you, Mom!

This book is dedicated to
Hattie Lee Hawk Williams my beautiful
Granny. Thanks for teaching me how to
put LOVE into my food. Your spirit
will always live in my heart.
You are my Master Chef!

Table of Contents

My Southern Recipes

Let's Get This Party Started!

Sunday Brunch

Sunday Suppers

My Southern Recipes

Cookout At My House

Sweet Endings

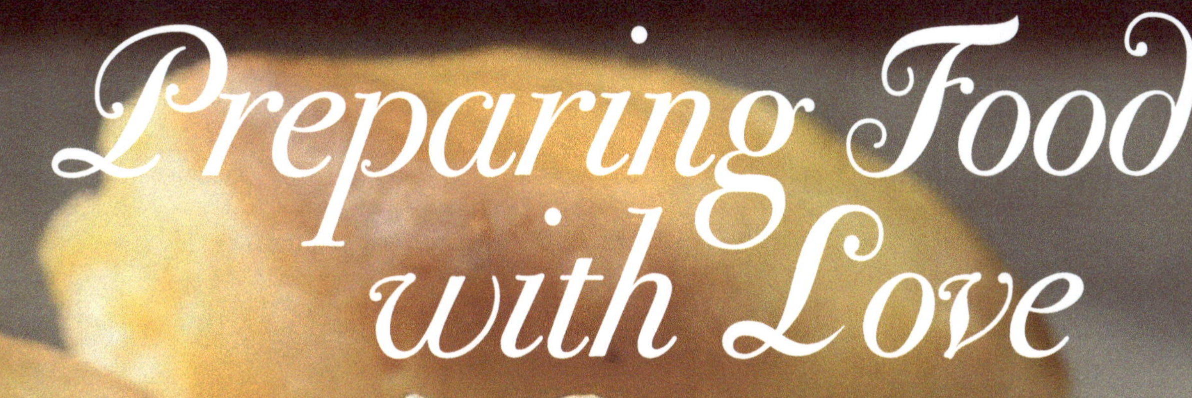
Preparing Food
with Love

Let's Get This Party Started!

Spicy Hot Wings

MAKES 2-4 SERVINGS

- 2 Lbs chicken wings
- 1/2 Cup flour
- 1/4 Tsp salt
- 1/4 Cup cayenne pepper
- Vegetable, frying oil
- 1/4 Cup butter
- 1/4 Cup of hot sauce*

Combine flour, salt and cayenne pepper in brown paper bag. Dot wings dry with a paper towel. Shake wings in bag with flour mixture. Heat oil to 350°. You will need enough oil to deep fry wings in medium sauce pot. Fry lightly breaded wings in oil for 15 minutes. Remove wings and drain on paper towel.

Combine butter and hot sauce in a bowl and microwave for 1 minute until sauce is creamy when stirred. Combine wings with sauce, tossing in a large bowl. Serve hot wings with bleu cheese dressing and celery sticks.

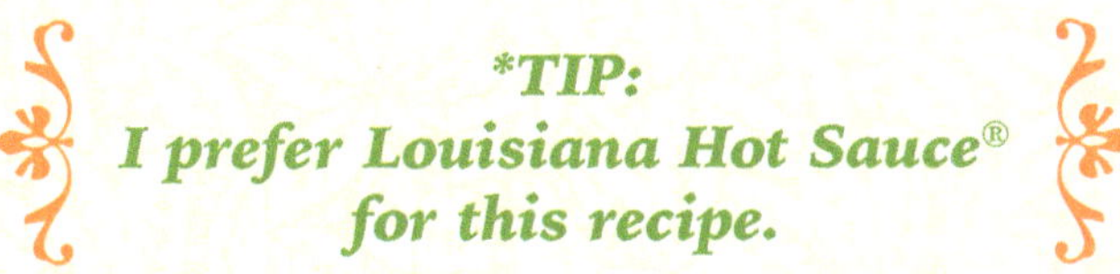

TIP:
I prefer Louisiana Hot Sauce® for this recipe.

Bleu Cheese Dressing

- 1/2 Cup mayonnaise
- 1/4 Cup whole milk
- 1/4 Cup sour cream
- Dash of salt and pepper
- 1/3 Cup bleu cheese crumbles

In a medium sized bowl, add mayonnaise, milk, sour cream and salt and pepper. Stir until combined and add bleu cheese. Stir until combined.

The first time I made hog's head cheese, I had to consult both my granny and my Aunt Doris. It was awful. I made it again and it was delicious. I was able to take some of what my granny said and some of what Aunt Doris said and develop it into what has become a winter favorite of family and clients. Hog's head cheese has become a delicacy that is served on charcuterie trays in upscale restaurants. Although you have to use a real hog's head, which you can only get from the actual slaughterhouse or an old-fashioned butcher.

Hog's Head Cheese

MAKES 10-12 SERVINGS

- **Fresh whole hog's head, split**
- **1 Lb pig ears**
- **1 Lb pig feet**
- **2 Large bell peppers, chopped**
- **3 Large onions, chopped**
- **1 Cup apple cider vinegar**
- **1 1/2 Tbsp crushed red pepper flakes**
- **1 Tbsp sage**
- **1 Tsp black pepper**
- **1 Tbsp salt**

Rinse off hog's head, pig ears and pig feet. Scrape off any hairs. Place in a large stock pot and cover with cold water.

Add the bell pepper, onions, vinegar, pepper flakes, sage, black pepper and salt. Simmer pot uncovered for 4 hours or until meat is very tender. Remove meat from the pot, reserving the leftover stock. Remove meat from the bones, discarding all the bones. Chop up all the meat into small chunks.

In a medium stock pot, add the meat and enough of the cooking liquid (stock) to cover the meat by about 1 inch. Bring hog's head mixture to a simmer. Taste and adjust seasoning and spices to your taste.

Add plastic wrap to two loaf pans (9 x 5 x 3). Pour hog's head mixture into pans and refrigerate until firm. Remove from loaf pans onto serving platters. Slice and serve with crackers.

Sausage Balls

MAKES 4 DOZEN

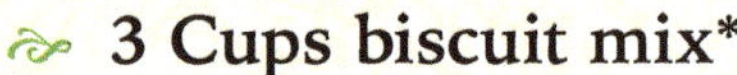

- 3 Cups biscuit mix*
- 1 Lb whole hog sausage (mild)
- 1 Lb cheddar cheese

Mix all ingredients well. Form into 1 inch balls. Bake at 325° for 20 minutes.

Cheese Ball

MAKES 8-10 SERVINGS

- 2 – 8 Oz cream cheese at room temperature
- 1 – 8 1/2 Oz can crushed pineapple
- 2 Cups chopped toasted pecans, divided
- 1/4 Cup chopped green pepper
- 1 Tbsp salt

Mix everything together, except 1 cup of nuts. Form into a ball and chill. Roll in remainder of pecans. Serve with Crackers.

Stewed Turkey Wings

MAKES 4 SERVINGS

- 3 Lbs turkey wings
- 1 Cup onion, chopped
- 1 Cup celery, chopped
- 1 Cup green bell pepper
- 1 Tbsp seasoning salt
- 1 Tsp black pepper
- 1 Tsp granulated garlic
- 1/2 Stick butter
- 2 Tbsp flour
- Water

In a large stock pot add turkey wings, then all other ingredients, except for flour. Cover ingredients with water. Bring to a boil, then lower temperatures, cover and simmer for 2 1/2 hours or until turkey wings are tender.

Place flour and 1/4 cup water in cup and mix well. Pour flour mixture into turkey wings. Stir and cook for another 20 minutes. Serve wings and sauce over rice.

Cajun Fried Pig Ears

MAKES 4 SERVINGS

- 6 pig ears
- 1 Small onion, chopped
- 3 Stalks celery
- 1/4 Cup vinegar
- 1/2 Tbsp seasoning salt
- 1 Tsp granulated garlic
- 1 Tsp black pepper
- Water
- 2 Cups flour
- 1 Quart of vegetable oil, for deep frying
- Cajun seasoning

Add the first 8 ingredients to a large stock pot. Cover with water, by 1 inch over. Bring to a boil, then lower heat and simmer for 4 hours until ears are tender. Remove ears from pot and allow to cool.

Cut ears into thin strips. Roll into flour and deep fry until brown and crispy (about 7 minutes). Do not overload fryer. Remove and drain on paper towels. Sprinkle with cajun seasoning.

Deviled Eggs

MAKES 12 SERVINGS

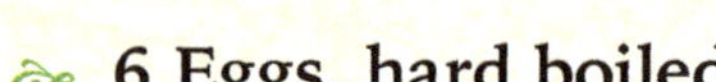

- 6 Eggs, hard boiled
- 1 Tsp yellow mustard
- 2 Tbsp mayonnaise
- 2 Tbsp pickled relish
- 1/4 Tsp salt
- Pinch of black pepper
- Pinch of cayenne pepper
- Paprika for sprinkling

Cut eggs in half on the long side. Remove yolks, leaving the whites intact. Combine egg yolks, mustard, mayo, relish, salt and peppers. Mix very well. Spoon mixture into egg whites and Sprinkle top of eggs lightly with paprika. Serve immediately, or refrigerate and serve cold.

See below for toppings recipes.

Crab Deviled Egg Topping

- 1 Cup imitation crabmeat, chopped
- 2 Tbsp mayonnaise
- 1/2 Tsp seafood seasoning spices
- 1 Tsp lemon juice
- 1/4 Tsp cayenne pepper

Mix all ingredients together. Add crab mixture to the top of each deviled egg.

Cajun Shrimp Deviled Egg Topping

- 12 Jumbo shrimp
- 2 Tsp seafood seasoning spices*
- 2 Tbsp butter

Season shrimp with the seafood seasoning spices. In a skillet, melt butter and add shrimp. Sauté for 2 minutes on both sides. Remove from pan and allow to cool. Add one shrimp to the top of each deviled eggs.

Baked Spinach Artichoke Dip

MAKES 8 SERVINGS

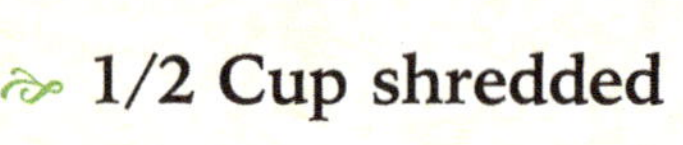

- 1/2 Cup shredded mozzarella cheese
- 1/2 Cup sour cream
- 1/2 Cup mayonnaise
- 1/2 Cup parmesan cheese, grated, divided
- 1 – 14 Oz can artichoke hearts, drained and chopped
- 1 Cup spinach leaves, chopped

In a large bowl, combine mozzarella cheese, sour cream, mayonnaise and 1/4 cup of parmesan cheese. Stir in artichoke and spinach. Spread mixture into a 9-inch pie plate. Sprinkle with the remaining 1/4 cup parmesan cheese.

Bake uncovered in a 350° oven for 15 minutes. Serve with crackers.

Spinach Dip

MAKES 8-10 SERVINGS

- 1 Package frozen chopped spinach, cooked
- 1 Package vegetable soup mix
- 1 – 8 Oz carton sour cream
- 1 Cup mayonnaise
- Dash of hot sauce*

Drain the spinach well by removing all the moisture. Stir the ingredients together and chill thoroughly. Serve with your favorite bread. A hallowed out bread bowl makes for a nice presentation, try using white mountain bread and carefully cut the center and pull out the soft pieces and set aside.

TIP:
I have several types of hot sauce in my pantry. However, Louisiana Hot Sauce® is one of my favorites!

Hot Crab Dip

MAKES 6-8 SERVINGS

- 2 – 8 Oz packages of cream cheese, softened
- 1/4 Cup mayonnaise
- 2 Cups of sharp cheddar cheese, shredded
- 1 Lb crab meat
- 1 Tsp lemon pepper
- 1 Tsp granulated garlic
- 1 Tsp seafood seasoning spices*
- 2 Tbsp fresh lemon juice

Preheat oven to 350°. In a medium bowl, combine all ingredients. Transfer to a 9 x 13 inch baking dish. Bake for 30 minutes, until golden brown. Serve with crackers.

Watermelon Spritzer

MAKES 4 SERVINGS

- 3 Lbs of watermelon, seedless, cubed
- 3 Whole lemons, juiced
- 1/2 Cup sugar (extra fine)
- 2 Cups ginger ale

Place watermelon, lemon juice and sugar into a food processor. Process until smooth. Strain mixture into a large bowl. Pour juice into a large pitcher and chill. Add ginger ale before serving.

Mock Sangria

MAKES 8-10 SERVINGS

- 1/4 Cup sugar
- 1 Cup orange juice
- 4 Cups grape juice
- 1/2 Fresh lemon, sliced
- 1/2 Cup fresh pineapple, chunked
- 1/2 Fresh orange, sliced
- 1 Small apple, cut in wedges
- 4 Cups ginger ale

In a large pitcher, combine sugar, orange juice and grape juice. Stir well. Add cut fruit. Refrigerate for 1 hour and add ginger ale just before serving.

Hot Chocolate

MAKES 4 SERVINGS

- 2 Oz semisweet chocolate pieces
- 1/3 Cup sugar
- 4 Cups whole milk

In a medium saucepan, combine chocolate, sugar and 1/2 cup of milk. Stir over medium heat until mixture comes to a light boil. Stir in remaining 3 1/2 cups of milk. Heat through but do not boil.

Remove from heat. If desired, top with marshmallows or whipped topping.

Strawberry Milkshake

MAKES 2 SERVINGS

- 1 Pint strawberry ice cream
- 1/2 Cup whole milk
- 1/2 Cup strawberries, hulled and chopped

Place all ingredients in a blender. Cover and blend until smooth. Serve immediately.

Fresh Squeezed Lemonade

MAKES 4 SERVINGS

- 1 1/2 Cup fresh squeezed lemon juice (8 – 10 lemons)
- 1 Cup sugar
- 6 Cups of water

Stir all ingredients until sugar is dissolved. Serve over ice. Garnish with lemon wheels.

Raspberry Lemonade

MAKES 8 SERVINGS

- 1/2 Cup fresh or frozen raspberries
- 9 Cups water
- 2 Cups freshly squeezed lemon juice (10 – 12 lemons)
- 2 Cups sugar

Puree raspberries in a blender and strain through a fine sieve into a pitcher. Add remaining ingredients and stir until sugar dissolves. Refrigerate and serve over ice, garnished with fresh raspberries and lemon wheels.

Fried Green Tomatoes

MAKES 8-10 SERVINGS

- **4 Green tomatoes, cut in 1/4 inch rings**
- **2 Cups self-rising flour**
- **2 Cups** panko **bread crumbs**
- **Paprika**
- **Salt**
- **Pepper**
- **2 Eggs**
- **1 Cup of whole milk**
- **Vegetable oil**

Season tomatoes on both sides with salt and pepper. Place flour in a shallow pan and season with paprika, salt and pepper. In another shallow pan season bread crumbs with paprika, salt and pepper. In a third shallow pan beat together milk and eggs.

Dredge tomato slices in flour, egg wash and then panko crumbs. Fry in vegetable oil until golden brown on both sides. Serve immediately.

For dipping sauce, try serving this with our Spicy Remoulade Sauce. *See the recipe on page 58.*

Fried Pickles

MAKES 4 SERVINGS

- 1 Quart of dill pickles, thinly sliced
- 1 Cup all purpose flour
- 2 Tsp red pepper
- 2 Tsp Spanish paprika
- 2 Tsp black pepper
- 1 Tsp salt
- 2 Eggs, beaten
- 2 Tbsp hot sauce
- Vegetable oil

Combine flour and spices together. Combine eggs and hot sauce together, whisking until fluffy. Dredge pickles into flour mixture, then in egg mixture then back into flour mixture.

Deep fry in vegetable oil at 375° until pickles are golden brown. Drain on paper towels. Serve immediately.

Try serving this with our Spicy Remoulade Sauce on page 58.

Pineapple Cheese Casserole

MAKES 6-8 SERVINGS

- **20 Oz pineapple tidbits**
- **1/2 Cup sugar**
- **3 Tbsp all purpose flour**
- **3 Tbsp pineapple juice**
- **1 Cup shredded sharp cheddar cheese**
- **1/4 Cup butter, melted**
- **1/2 Cup cracker crumbs**

Drain pineapple, reserving 3 tbsp of the juice. Combine sugar, flour and juice. Add cheese and pineapple tidbits. Stir well. Spoon into greased 1 quart casserole and Combine melted butter and cracker crumbs. Sprinkle over pineapple mixture.

Bake at 350° for 20 to 30 minutes until golden brown and bubbly.

Sunday Brunch

Chicken and Smoked Sausage Gumbo

MAKES 10-12 SERVINGS

- 1 Cup vegetable oil
- 1 Cup flour
- 2 Cups onion, chopped
- 1 Cup bell pepper, chopped
- 1 Cup celery, chopped
- 4 Quarts chicken stock
- 2 Tsp creole seasoning
- 2 Bay leaves
- Salt & pepper
- 4 Large chicken breasts, cut in large cubes
- 2 Lbs smoked sausage, cut into half inch slices

In large, heavy bottom pot, heat oil and cook the flour in the oil over medium to high heat, stirring constantly, until the roux reaches a deep brown color, watching carefully not to burn it.

Add the vegetables and stir. Cook for a few minutes then add the stock, creole seasoning, bay leaves and salt & pepper. Add the chicken breast and sausage. Bring to a boil. Reduce heat to a simmer, and then cook for an hour. Remove bay leaf. Taste to adjust the seasoning as needed.

Serve over cooked rice if desired.

Lentil and Sausage Soup

MAKES 4 SERVINGS

- 1 Lb italian sausage
- 1 Large onion, chopped
- 1/2 Cup green pepper
- 6 Cups chicken broth
- 1 Can (14 1/2 oz) of diced tomatoes, undrained
- 1 Tsp salt
- 1 Tsp granulated garlic
- 1 Tsp fresh ground pepper
- 2 Cups dry lentils, rinsed

Brown sausage in a large stock pot. Add onion and peppers. Sauté for 2 minutes. Add remaining ingredients and cook for about 1 hour or until lentils are tender. Taste and adjust seasoning with salt and pepper.

Loaded Baked Potato Soup

MAKES 4-6 SERVINGS

- 1/2 Cup butter
- 1/2 Cup onion, chopped
- 1/2 Cup celery
- 3/4 Cup flour
- 5 Cups whole milk
- 1 Cup chicken broth
- 1 1/2 Cups shredded sharp cheddar cheese
- 4 Large idaho potatoes; baked, peeled and cut into chunks
- 12 Slices bacon, cooked and crumbled
- 1 Cup sour cream
- Salt and pepper

Melt butter in a large dutch oven over medium heat; add onion and celery and sauté until tender. Add flour to mixture and cook flour for 4 minutes, stirring constantly.

Whisk in milk and chicken broth, whisking until mixture thickens. Add cheese, potatoes, bacon and sour cream. Stir well and cook until heated through. Taste and season with salt and pepper to taste.

Corn and Crab Chowder

MAKES 8-10 SERVINGS

- 1 Small onion, diced
- 2 Stalks of celery, diced
- 1 Stick of butter
- 3/4 Cup of flour
- 1 Tsp seafood seasoning spices*
- 1 Tsp granulated garlic
- 2 Chicken bouillon cubes
- 1 Quart whole milk
- 1 Pint heavy cream
- 1 1/2 Cups of frozen corn
- 5 Medium russet potatoes, peeled, diced and cooked – al dente
- 1 Lb of crab meat, lump or claw
- Salt and pepper

In medium pot, sauté onion and celery in butter until onions are translucent. Turn heat to low and add flour. Stir well. Add seafood seasoning spices, garlic powder, and chicken bouillon. Stir. Whisk in milk and cream.

Bring to a light simmer. Add potatoes and corn. Stir and bring to a light simmer. Gently fold in crab meat. Add salt and pepper to taste. Simmer for 10 minutes on low. Serve hot.

TIP:
I prefer Old Bay Seasoning® for most of my seafood dishes.

Grilled Cheese Sandwich

MAKES 2 SERVINGS

- **4 Slices white bread**
- **3 Tbsp of butter, divided and softened**
- **2 Slices of cheddar cheese**
- **2 Slices of pepper jack cheese**

Preheat skillet over medium heat. Generously butter one side of a slice of bread. Place bread buttered side down onto skillet. Add 1 slice of each cheese. Butter a second slice of bread on one side. Place bread buttered side up on top of the sandwich.

Grill until lightly browned. Flip over. Continue grilling until cheese is melted. Lower heat if bread is cooking too fast. Repeat process.

Tomato Soup

MAKES 4 SERVINGS

- 1 Can (14 oz) chopped tomatoes
- 3/4 Cup vegetable oil, divided
- Salt and fresh ground pepper
- 1/2 Cup celery, diced
- 1/2 Cup carrots, diced
- 1 Cup onion, diced
- 3 Garlic cloves, minced
- 1 Cup chicken broth
- 1/4 Cup fresh basil
- 1/4 Cup heavy cream

Preheat oven to 375°.

Strain the chopped canned tomatoes, reserving the juices. Spread tomatoes onto a baking sheet. Season with salt and pepper. Drizzle with 1/4 cup of oil. Roast until caramelized (about 15 to 20 minutes).

Meanwhile, in a saucepan, heat remaining oil on medium heat. Add celery, carrots, onion and garlic. Cook until softened. Add roasted tomatoes, tomato juice and chicken broth. Simmer for 30 minutes. Puree mixture with an immersion blender until smooth. Add basil and heavy cream. Blend again slightly.

Quick Chili

MAKES 4 SERVINGS

- 1 Lb ground beef
- 1/2 Cup onion
- 1/2 Cup bell pepper
- 1 Tsp seasoning salt
- 3 Tbsp chili powder
- 1 Tbsp ground cumin
- 2 – 14 1/2 Oz can stewed tomatoes
- 2 Cans kidney beans
- 3 Tbsp hot sauce
- 1 Tbsp sugar
- Salt and pepper

Brown beef in large skillet and drain oil. Add onion, bell pepper, seasoning salt, chili powder, and cumin. Cook until onions are translucent. Add tomatoes, kidney beans, hot sauce and sugar.

Cook for 45 minutes on low heat. Add salt and pepper to taste.

Try serving with our Crackling Cornbread on page 74.

Gourmet Ramen Noodles (Ghetto Pho)

MAKES 2 SERVINGS

- 1 Tbsp butter
- 1/2 Onion, diced small
- 2 Garlic cloves, crushed
- 2 Scallion stalks, thinly sliced
- 2 Tbsp soy sauce
- 3 Cups chicken broth
- 6 Oz cooked chicken, cut in chunks (rotisserie works well)
- 2 – 8 Oz packs dried instant ramen noodles
- 2 Eggs
- 2 Tbsp vegetable oil
- Salt and pepper

In a medium saucepan, melt the butter. Add the onions, garlic, white part of the scallions (save the green for garnish). Sauté until onions are translucent. Add soy sauce and chicken broth then simmer for 10 minutes. Add chicken and continue to simmer on low while you prepare the noodles and fry the egg *(see below)*.

FRIED EGG: Heat skillet and add vegetable oil. Crack eggs in the skillet. Add salt and pepper to eggs and cook until whites are done but yolk is still runny. You can flip it and cook it longer, if your taste buds prefer hard fried eggs.

Boil the noodles for 3 minutes or until al dente. Drain and add to broth. Top with fried egg and green part of the scallion.

Bacon Honey Hoe Cakes

MAKES
10-12 SERVINGS

- 4 Cups self-rising cornmeal
- 4 Eggs
- 4 Tbsp sugar
- 2 1/2 Cups whole milk
- 1/2 Cup vegetable oil
- 1/2 Cup cooked bacon and bacon fat drippings
- Honey

Mix all ingredients except the honey together until smooth. Cook round cakes on a well-greased hot griddle.

Drizzle lightly with honey.

French Toast

MAKES 4 SERVINGS

- 4 Beaten eggs
- 1 Cup whole milk
- 2 Tbsp sugar
- 2 Tsp vanilla
- 1/2 Tsp cinnamon
- 8 Slices white bread
- Butter or margarine
- Maple syrup

In a shallow bowl, beat together eggs, milk, sugar, vanilla and cinnamon. Dip bread slices into egg mixture, coating both sides.

In a skillet or griddle melt butter or margarine over medium heat. Add bread slices and cook 2 to 3 minutes per side or until golden brown. Serve warm with syrup.

Sweet Potato Waffles

MAKES 6 WAFFLES

- 1 1/2 Cups sweet potatoes, peeled and cubed
- 2 Cups all purpose flour
- 1 Tsp baking powder
- 1/4 Tsp nutmeg
- 1/2 Tsp salt
- 6 Egg whites
- 1 Cup whole milk
- 1/4 Cup light brown sugar
- 1/4 Cup melted butter
- 1 Tsp vanilla

Boil potatoes for about 20 minutes until fork tender. Mash cooked potatoes and set aside.

In a separate container, combine flour, baking powder, nutmeg and salt.

Beat egg whites until stiff peaks form. Set aside.

In another bowl, combine sweet potatoes, milk, brown sugar, butter and vanilla. Stir the sweet potato mixture into the flour mixture and thoroughly combine. Gradually fold egg whites into batter. The batter will be thick. Place 1/2 cup of batter onto a preheated, oiled waffle iron. Cook until lightly browned – 5 to 6 minutes.

Try these waffles with a pecan maple syrup *(see recipe below)*.

Pecan Maple Syrup

- 1/4 Cup chopped pecans
- 1 Cup maple syrup

Toast pecans in skillet. Add maple syrup slowly and bring syrup to a low simmer.

Hummingbird Waffles with Cream Cheese Butter

MAKES 6 WAFFLES

- 1 1/4 cups self-rising flour
- 3/4 Cup sugar
- 1/2 Cup chopped pecans
- 1/2 Tsp baking soda
- 1/4 Tsp cinnamon
- 1/4 Tsp nutmeg
- 1/4 Tsp salt
- 1 Cup smashed bananas
- 1/2 Cup vegetable oil
- 1/4 Cup crushed pineapple (drained)
- 1/4 Cup sour cream
- 1 Tsp vanilla
- 2 Large eggs, whisked until fluffy

Whisk together flour, sugar, pecans, baking soda, cinnamon, nutmeg, and salt in a large mixing bowl. Combine bananas, oil, pineapple, sour cream, vanilla and eggs in another bowl. Fold the banana mixture into the flour mixture until just combined. The mixture will be lumpy.

Grease or spray heated waffle iron with oil. Add batter to iron and cook until golden brown, about 4 minutes. Spread with cream cheese butter *(see recipe below)* and powdered sugar or your favorite maple syrup.

Cream Cheese Butter

- 1 – 8 Oz package cream cheese (softened)
- 1/2 Stick butter (softened)
- 2 Tbsp powdered sugar

Combine ingredients in a mixing bowl. With a hand mixer, beat on low speed until mixture is light and fluffy.

Blueberry Muffins

MAKES 12 MUFFINS

- 1 Stick butter, softened
- 1 Cup sugar
- 2 Eggs
- 1 Tsp vanilla extract
- 2 Tsp baking powder
- 1/4 Tsp salt
- 2 Cups flour
- 1/2 Cup whole milk
- 2 Cups fresh or frozen blueberries

Preheat oven to 375°. Grease a muffin tin or line the cups with paper liners. With a mixer, cream the butter until smooth. Add sugar and mix. Add the eggs, vanilla, baking powder, and salt. Mix well.

With the mixer on low, add 1/2 the flour, then 1/2 of the milk and mix. Repeat with remaining flour and milk. Fold in blueberries by hand until well mixed. Fill muffin cups 3/4 full. Sprinkle tops with sugar and bake for 25 to 30 minutes until golden brown. Let cool slightly then remove from muffin tin.

Grandma Mobley's biscuits are like no other. Those were the best biscuits I have ever had. The first time I met Grandma Mobley was at a holiday dinner where I found her busy making biscuits in the kitchen. I asked her if she would show me how she made them. When I tried them for the first time, they were nothing like hers. I later learned from her daughter, Aunt Gloria, that she started making biscuits at the age of 7, and she made them almost every day until she passed away at age 80. So, don't be discouraged if they're not great the first time. Try them again, and keep on trying them. They really are great biscuits!

Grandma Mobley's Old Fashioned Biscuits

MAKES 12 BISCUITS

- 2 Cups self-rising flour
- 1/4 Cup shortening, cold*
- 1 Cup evaporated milk, cold
- 2 Tbsp melted butter

Preheat oven to 400°. Put flour in a bowl. With a fork, stir in the shortening until it forms crumbles. Pour in evaporated milk and mix gently until dough is formed.

Roll out the dough to 1/2 inch thickness on a floured board. Cut with a 2 inch cutter. Brush tops with melted butter. Bake on a greased baking sheet for 10 minutes or until lightly brown. Brush tops again with melted butter.

***TIP:**
I prefer Crisco® Shortening when I make homemade biscuits.

Easy Strawberry Jam

MAKES 12 SERVINGS

- **5 Cups crushed strawberries**
- **1/4 Cup lemon juice**
- **6 Tbsp real fruit pectin**
- **7 Cups sugar**

Combine strawberries and lemon juice in a large saucepot. Gradually stir in pectin. Bring mixture to a rolling boil, stirring constantly.

Add sugar, stirring to dissolve. Boil for 1 minute, stirring constantly. Remove from heat and skim off any foam that has formed on the top.

To extend jam's shelf life, process in canning jars according to manufacturer's instructions.

Easy Peaches and Biscuits (Dumplings)

MAKES 8-10 SERVINGS

- **29 Oz can sliced peaches in heavy syrup**
- **1 Stick of butter**
- **2 Cups sugar**
- **1 Tsp vanilla**
- **Pinch nutmeg**
- **2 Cans plain biscuits**

In large pot, add peaches and heavy syrup. Fill empty can with water and add to pot. Add butter, sugar, vanilla, and nutmeg. Bring to a boil. Pinch off 1/2 inch sized balls of biscuit dough and drop into mixture – stirring frequently.

While peach broth is boiling, lower heat. Simmer on low for 15 minutes or until dumplings are done.

Shrimp Cakes

MAKES 4-6 SERVINGS

- **20 Large shrimp (1 lb), peeled and deveined**
- **1 Large egg**
- **2 Tbsp shallots, chopped finely**
- **2 Tbsp fresh lemon juice**
- **1/2 Tsp hot sauce**
- **1/2 Tbsp seafood seasoning spices***
- **2 Cups panko bread crumbs**
- **Vegetable oil**

Coarsely chop shrimp in food processor. Add egg, shallots, lemon juice, hot sauce, and seafood seasoning spices. Pulse processor. Add 1 cup of panko bread crumbs and blend, just until combined. Roll shrimp cakes in remaining 1 cup of panko bread crumbs (3 inch cakes). Refrigerate for 10 minutes to set.

Heat oil in large skillet. Pan fry cakes until cooked through and golden brown on both sides, about 6 minutes. Drain on paper towels.

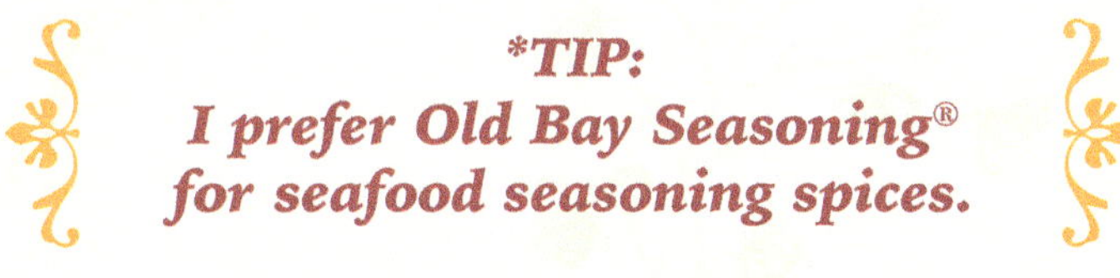

Blue Crab Crab Cakes

MAKES 12 PATTIES

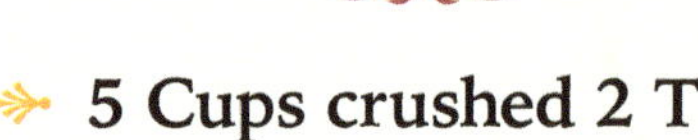

- **5 Cups crushed 2 Tbsp red bell pepper, diced small**
- **2 Tbsp green bell pepper, diced small**
- **2 Tbsp butter**
- **1 Lb of blue crab (picked over for shells)**
- **1 Egg**
- **1 Tsp sugar**
- **1/4 Tsp seafood seasoning spices***
- **1/4 Cup panko bread crumbs**
- **1 Tbsp mayonnaise**

Sauté bell peppers with butter until tender. Combine remaining ingredients and add sautéed peppers. Roll into 2 inch patties and bake on a greased sheet pan at 350° for 15 minute or until golden brown.

***TIP:**
Use your favorite seafood spice or try using Old Bay Seasoning®*

Spicy Remoulade Sauce

Place all ingredients in a small mixing bowl. Stir until smooth. Let sit for 15 minutes and stir again. Chill until ready to serve.

MAKES 6-8 SERVINGS

- **1 1/2 Cups mayonnaise**
- **1 Tbsp granulated garlic**
- **2 Tbsp hot sauce***
- **1 Tbsp seafood seasoning spices***
- **1/4 Cup fresh squeezed lemon juice**
- **2 Tbsp sugar**
- **1 Tsp seasoning salt***
- **1/4 Tsp cayenne pepper**

This is the best recipe for crab cakes. A lot of times there is too much focus on the amount of crab meat that is in a crab cake. Or, when crab meat is not available in excess, there is too much breading in the crab cake. Balancing the crab meat and the breading is the key. It's called a crab cake for a reason – crab AND bread (cake).

***TIP:**
I make my remoulade sauce with the following: Old Bay®, and Louisiana Hot Sauce®.*

Crispy Whole Red Snapper with Asian Ponzu Sauce

MAKES 2 SERVINGS

- 1/2 Onion, diced small
- 3 Cloves garlic, minced
- 2 Tbsp sesame oil
- 1 Cup asian ponzu sauce
- 1/4 Cup soy sauce
- 1 Tsp rice vinegar
- 1 Tbsp fish sauce
- 1 Tbsp chili garlic sauce
- 1 1/2 Cups water
- 3 Tbsp honey
- 2 Tbsp cornstarch mixed with 1/2 cup water
- 2 Whole red snappers, 1–2 lbs.
- Salt and pepper
- 1 Cup of cornstarch
- 2 Cups flour
- Vegetable oil for deep frying

Sauté onions and garlic in sesame oil until translucent and add ponzu, soy sauce, rice vinegar, fish sauce, chili garlic sauce, water and honey. Simmer for 10 minutes. Combine cornstarch with water. Mix well. Whisk into ponzu mixture. Cook for 5 minutes.

Make slits into fish, season with salt and pepper and dredge into combined cornstarch and flour mixture. Deep fry in vegetable oil at 350° for 7 to 10 minutes. Drain on paper towels, pour ponzu sauce on fried fish and serve immediately.

Chicken Liver Custard

MAKES 6 SERVINGS

- 2 Cups chicken broth (low sodium)
- 8 Oz fresh chicken livers
- 1/4 Tsp kosher salt
- 1/4 Tsp fresh ground pepper
- 4 Eggs
- 1/4 Cup soy sauce
- 1 Cup chicken broth
- 1 Tbsp cornstarch
- 6 Strips of bacon, baked crispy and crumbled

In processor or blender blend chicken broth and chicken livers together. Add salt and pepper. Blend for 20 seconds, until smooth. Add eggs one at a time and pulse quickly to keep mixture from foaming up. Pulse until the mixture has a smooth texture.

Strain chicken livers custard through a fine mesh sieve into a medium bowl. Ladle custard into 6 ramekins. Place in a baking pan and add hot water to reach halfway up the cups. Cover with foil tightly. Bake for 20 minutes or until set in the center.

Heat soy sauce and chicken broth combined with cornstarch together, whisking until slightly thickened. Top with soy sauce mixture and bacon crumbles.

Mayport Shrimp and Grits

MAKES 8-10 SERVINGS

GRITS

- 3 cups water
- 1 cup of grits
- 1/2 tsp salt
- 2 tbsp butter
- 1/3 cup heavy cream
- 1/4 cup sharp cheddar cheese

Use a heavy bottom sauce pot and add salt to the water. Bring the water to a rapid boil. Whisk in the grits and stir really well. Lower the heat and cook for 20 minutes, add butter, heavy cream, and cheddar cheese, stir well.

Mayport shrimp is some of the best in the world. But using fresh shrimp from your grocer would make this recipe tasty as well.

SHRIMP

- 1 Lb mayport shrimp (tail on, shell off, deveined)
- 3 Oz butter
- 1/4 Cup smoked ham, cut into small cubes
- 1/3 Cup bell peppers (red or green)
- 1/3 Cup onions
- 2 Tbsp flour
- 2 Cups water
- 1 Tsp seafood base
- 1/2 Tsp black pepper
- 1/2 Tsp seafood seasoning spices*
- 1 Tbsp granulated garlic
- 1/3 Cup heavy cream

Cook shrimp in butter until they turn pink, 3 minutes on each side and remove shrimp from pan. Add ham, peppers and onions to pan. Cook for 2 minutes and add flour. Stir for 2 minutes. Add seafood base to water and stir. Add to pan along with pepper, seafood seasoning spices, and garlic.

Let sauce cook until thickened and reduced. Add heavy cream at the end. Return shrimp to the pan. Serve over grits.

The addition of heavy cream at the end gives your grits a flavorful creamy goodness that takes the dining experience to a whole new level. The cream is not just about the creaminess. The flavor that the heavy cream adds will make grit lovers hum.

Salmon Croquettes

MAKES 4 SERVINGS

- 1/4 Cup finely diced onion
- 1/4 Cup finely diced bell peppers
- 1/2 Stick of butter
- 1 – 16 Oz can pink salmon
- 1 Egg
- 1/4 Cup corn meal (self-rising)
- 1 Dash of salt
- 1 Tsp black pepper
- 1 1/2 Cups vegetable oil

Sauté onion and bell peppers in butter until translucent. Drain salmon; remove bones if desired. In a medium mixing bowl, mix salmon, egg and onion mixture. Stir in corn meal, season with salt and pepper.

Form into small sphere shaped patties and fry in hot oil until deep brown 5 minutes on each side.

Southern Fried Chicken

MAKES 4-6 SERVINGS

- 1 Chicken, cut into 8 pieces
- 2 Tsp salt
- 1 1/2 Tsp pepper
- 1 Tsp granulated garlic
- 1 Tsp paprika
- 1 Cup flour
- 1 Tsp paprika
- 2 Cups vegetable oil

Clean chicken and drain off excess water. In a bowl, combine chicken with salt, pepper, and granulated garlic. Let chicken sit for a few minutes.

Mix flour and paprika in a brown paper bag. Place 2 to 3 pieces of chicken in the bag and shake until each piece is coated with flour.

In a large cast iron skillet, heat oil until it reaches 350° or until it bubbles when flour is sprinkled into it. Add the chicken but do not overcrowd the pan. Reduce heat to 325°. Cook chicken for 7 minutes, checking it in between to make sure it's not burning. Turn chicken over and cook for an additional 5 to 7 minutes, or until the thigh center juices run clear. Remove from the skillet and drain on paper towels.

Chicken should reach an internal temperature of 165°.

Granny's fried chicken was really simple. She did not marinate it in buttermilk or use some fancy brine. However the chicken must be fresh and not frozen. I promise you it is simply delicious! When you first put the chicken in the oil, the bubbles rise up like rolling waves. As the chicken cooks, the bubbles subside, which lets you know the chicken is almost ready. Using a cast iron skillet helps to control the temperature better. But, the secret is in the brown paper bag. So, next time the grocery store clerk asks you if plastic is ok, tell her NO!

Pulled Pork Sliders

MAKES 16 SERVINGS

- 3 Lbs pork roast
- 2 Tbsp paprika
- 1 Tbsp granulated garlic
- 1 Tbsp black pepper
- 1 Tbsp lemon pepper seasoning
- 1 1/2 Cups of chicken stock
- 1 1/2 Cups of barbecue sauce*
- 16 Slider rolls

Preheat oven to 225°. Score pork roast. Combine all seasoning in a bowl. Massage seasonings into meat. Place roast in a roasting pan and pour chicken stock into the pan. Cover with foil and roast for 3 hours.

Remove the foil and continue to cook until the pork has reached 190° (about 1 1/2 hours more). Rest for 30 minutes. Pull pork into long shreds using 2 forks. Get rid of the fat. Toss the pork with any leftover juices and barbecue sauce. Serve on slider rolls. Top with fried pickles (optional). *See recipe on page 32.*

***TIP:**
I prefer Sweet Baby Ray's® Barbecue Sauce.*

Rum Balls

MAKES 3 1/2 DOZEN

- 3 Cups (1 box) vanilla wafers, finely crushed
- 2 Cups powdered sugar
- 1 Cup nuts (optional)
- 1/4 Cup cocoa powder*
- 1/2 Cup light rum*
- 1/4 Cup light corn syrup

Mix all ingredients together. Make approximately 1 inch balls and roll in powdered sugar. Place in container and refrigerate for 2 days.

***TIPS:**
I prefer Hershey's® Cocoa Powder when I make homemade Rum Balls. Any light-colored rum will do, but I like Bacardi® Rum in this recipe. Your grocer may have their own version of a vanilla wafer, I like Nilla Wafer® brand.

I make these every year during the Thanksgiving and Christmas holiday season. There's just something about rum and chocolate. These delicious treats make a great gift along with the Pecan Rum Cake. Friends don't let friends drink and drive, but there's absolutely nothing wrong with having a rum ball. Rum, rum! Yum, yum!

Hot Toddy

MAKES 2-3 SERVINGS

- 1/2 Cup gin
- 1 1/2 Cup ginger tea (made from 2 ginger tea bags)
- 2 Tbsp honey
- 1/4 Cup peppermint liquor
- 1/4 Cup fresh squeezed lemon juice
- 1 Peppermint ball

Combine all the ingredients except for the peppermint ball, simmer for 10 minutes. Serve hot with a peppermint ball added.

For the record, my granny did not drink. But, in the wintertime, there was always the hot toddy mixture in the refrigerator, with a peppermint in it. Whenever cold season was on the horizon, granny would serve a hot toddy to ward off cold symptoms. An infamous part of the home remedy has always been to "sweat out" a cold. A hot toddy is best when you're planning to go to bed and snuggle under the covers. It will definitely cause you to sweat it out. And because it is used strictly for medicinal purposes, even a good Christian will drink it or administer it, or both.

Sunday Suppers

Cracklin' Cornbread

MAKES 6-8 SERVINGS

- **1 Cup self-rising cornmeal**
- **1/2 Cup self-rising flour**
- **2 Tbsp sugar**
- **2 Eggs, beaten**
- **1 1/4 Cups buttermilk**
- **3 Tbsp vegetable oil**
- **1 Cup cracklin'**

Preheat oven to 400°. In a bowl mix together cornmeal, flour and sugar. Add the eggs and buttermilk to flour mixture.

In a cast iron skillet add oil, heat the pan in the oven until smoking hot. Add the cracklin' to mixture and add mixture to hot pan. Bake for 25 to 30 minutes until brown. Cut into wedges.

It just doesn't get any more Southern than crackling cornbread. Cornbread or biscuits are always a part of a Southern meal. Adding crackling to the cornbread is surely a treat. The crackling serves as an added bonus for extra flavor.

Corny Cornbread

MAKES 6-8 SERVINGS

- 1 Box cornbread mix*
- 1/2 Cup canned cream corn
- 1/2 Cup canned whole kernel corn, drained
- 1/2 Stick butter, melted
- 8 Oz sour cream

Mix ingredients in order listed. Pour into lightly greased 13 x 9 pan. Bake at 350° for 30 minutes.

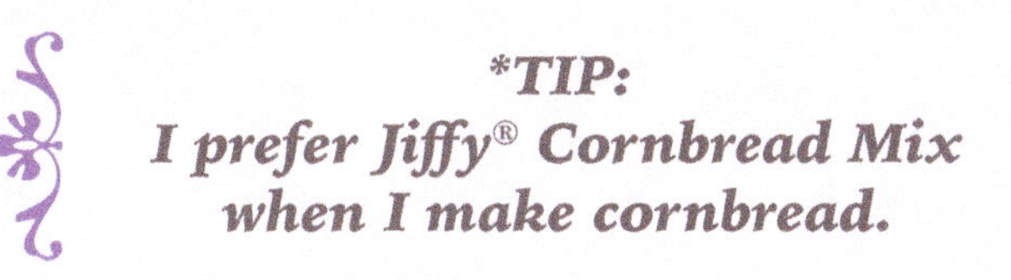

***TIP:**
I prefer Jiffy® Cornbread Mix when I make cornbread.

Hushpuppies

MAKES 20 2-INCH HUSHPUPPIES

- 1/2 Cup self-rising flour
- 1 Cup self-rising cornmeal
- 1 Tbsp sugar
- 2 Tbsp onions, minced
- 1 Egg, beaten
- 3/4 Cup buttermilk

Combine flour and cornmeal. Add sugar. Add onions. Stir in egg and buttermilk and let mixture sit for 5 minutes. Stir again. Heat oil to 350° and drop the batter into hot oil by the tablespoon and fry until brown all over. Drain on paper towel. Serve hot.

Sweet Potato Biscuits

MAKES 20 BISCUITS

- **2 Cups cooked, mashed sweet potatoes**
- **1 Stick of butter, melted**
- **1 1/4 Cups whole milk**
- **4 Cups self-rising flour**
- **Pinch baking soda**
- **3 Tbsp sugar**

Preheat oven to 400°. Boil the sweet potatoes until tender which takes about 30 minutes until they are fork tender. Remove them and let cool and then remove the skin.

Mix together sweet potatoes, butter, milk and mix until well blended. Stir in flour, sugar and baking soda. Knead into a ball on a floured area. Roll out dough into 1/2 inch thick after kneading about 8 times. Cut with 2 inch biscuit cutter. Bake in a greased baking pan for 10 minutes or until brown.

These biscuits are great when paired with our homemade cinnamon butter *(see recipe below)*.

Cinnamon Butter

- **12 Oz butter, room temperature**
- **3 Tbsp honey**
- **3 Tsp cinnamon**

In mixer, blend all ingredients together until creamy smooth.

Zucchini Bread

MAKES 2 LOAFS

- 3 Eggs
- 1 Cup vegetable oil
- 2 Tsp vanilla
- 2 Cups sugar
- 2 Cups grated zucchini
- 3 Cups flour
- 1 Tsp baking soda
- 1 Tsp salt
- 1 Cup chopped pecans or walnuts
- 1 Cup raisins (optional)

Beat eggs until light. Add oil, vanilla, sugar and zucchini. Mix well. Blend in dry ingredients. Stir in nuts and raisins. Bake in 2 greased 9 x 5 inch loaf pans on 350° for about 50 minutes.

Black-Eyed Peas

MAKES 4-6 SERVINGS

- 1/2 Lb bacon, cut in small strips
- 2 Tbsp vegetable oil
- 1/2 Onion
- 1 – 16 Oz package dried black eyed peas, rinsed
- 1 Hambone
- Salt and pepper, to taste

In a large saucepan cook bacon over low heat, until crisp. Add vegetable oil and onion. Cook until onions are translucent. Add black eyed peas and hambone. Cover peas with water and cook covered for 30 to 45 minutes, until peas are tender. Salt and pepper to taste.

For a thicker juice, smash a cup of peas and add them back to the pot. Stir and serve.

Butter Beans

MAKES 4 SERVINGS

- 2 Lbs butter beans (frozen)
- 2 Medium smoked pork neck bones
- 4 Cups water
- Salt and pepper

To a large stock pot, add butter peas and neck bones. Cover with water and bring to a boil. Reduce heat and simmer until beans are tender. Taste and add salt and pepper to your taste.

Seasoned Green Beans

MAKES 6-8 SERVINGS

- **4 Slices bacon, cut into pieces**
- **1/4 Cup onion, chopped**
- **1/4 Cup green bell peppers, cut into strips**
- **4 Cups water**
- **4 Chicken bouillon cubes**
- **1 Tsp black pepper**
- **2 Lbs string beans, ends trimmed**
- **3 Tbsp butter**

In a medium stock pot, cook the bacon until browned; remove bacon from the pot. Add onions and green bell peppers. Cook for 2 minutes.

Add water, chicken bouillon and black pepper. Bring to a simmer for 15 minutes. Add string beans and cook until tender but not mushy (about 30 minutes). Stir in butter. Top with cooked bacon. Serve.

Quick and Easy Broccoli Casserole

MAKES 6-8 SERVINGS

- 2 Boxes frozen chopped broccoli
- 1 Cup mayonnaise
- 1 Small can cream of mushroom soup
- 2 Eggs, beaten
- 1 Onion, chopped finely
- Salt and pepper
- 1 1/2 Cups grated sharp cheddar cheese
- 3 Tbsp margarine
- 2 Cups bread crumb stuffing mix

Cook broccoli according to package directions. Drain. Combine mayo, soup, eggs, onion, a pinch of salt and pepper. Add broccoli and pour into a 9 x 11 long casserole dish. Sprinkle cheese on top.

Melt margarine and combine with stuffing mix. Sprinkle on top of broccoli mixture. Bake at 350° for 45 minutes.

Macaroni and Cheese

MAKES 8-10 SERVINGS

- **2 Cups dried uncooked macaroni noodles**
- **2 Tbsp butter, melted**
- **2 Cups evaporated milk**
- **2 1/2 Cups sharp cheddar cheese (freshly grated), divided**
- **1/4 Cup shredded mozzarella cheese**
- **1 Can cheddar cheese soup**
- **1 Tsp salt**

Cook macaroni according to package directions. Drain. Set aside.

Return macaroni to the pot and add butter, milk, 2 cups sharp cheddar cheese, mozzarella cheese, cheddar cheese soup and salt. Stir until well combined. Spoon into a 2-quart casserole dish.

Top with remaining 1/2 cup of shredded cheddar cheese and bake for 30 minutes on 325° or until it bubbles and heated through. Let stand for 10 minutes before serving.

Mac and cheese is another Southern favorite that every family has a recipe for. But Mama's mac and cheese was always different. Now, you get to experience that difference. Fresh grated sharp cheddar cheese is the key. But, that's not all. Use cheese sauce instead of eggs. It serves as a binder to help hold everything together. Adding mozzarella cheese gives the dish a stringy cheesiness that makes it the cheesiest mac and cheese ever.

Carrot Souffle

MAKES 8-10 SERVINGS

- 3 Lbs carrots, peeled
- 2 Cups sugar
- 1 Tbsp baking powder
- 1 Tbsp vanilla extract
- 4 Tbsp flour
- 6 Eggs
- 2 Sticks butter, melted

Cook carrots until soft. While carrots are hot, mix with a hand mixer in a large mixing bowl. Add sugar, baking powder and vanilla. Mix until smooth.

Add flour and mix again until well combined. Mix in eggs and butter. Beat for 2 minutes. Place in an oven dish and bake at 350° for 1 1/2 hours.

Candied Yams

MAKES 4 SERVINGS

- 1/2 Stick butter
- 1 1/2 Cup sugar
- 1/4 Tsp nutmeg
- 1 Tsp vanilla extract
- 1/4 Cup water
- 3 Medium – large sweet potatoes, peeled and sliced in rounds

Melt butter in frying pan. Add all other ingredients except sweet potatoes. Stir mixture. Once sugar is dissolved, add sweet potatoes on top.

Cover and cook on medium low for 35 to 40 minutes. Sweet potatoes will make their own syrup.

Collard Green Risotto

MAKES 4 SERVINGS

- 2 Cups collard greens, cleaned and cut into strips
- 1 Medium onion, chopped
- 2 Cloves garlic, minced
- 2 Tbsp olive oil
- 1 Cup uncooked arborio rice
- 3 Cups of chicken broth
- 1/4 Cup finely shredded parmesan cheese
- 3 Tbsp parsley, chopped

In a large saucepan cook collards, onion and garlic in hot oil until onion is translucent. Add rice. Cook and stir over medium heat – about 5 minutes, until rice is light brown.

Meanwhile, in another saucepan bring broth to a boil. Reduce heat and simmer. Slowly add 1 cup of broth to the rice mixture, stirring constantly. Continue to cook and stir over medium heat until liquid is absorbed.

Add another 1/2 cup of the broth and repeat process until all broth has absorbed. Stir in parmesan cheese and parsley. Serve immediately.

There's nothing Southern about risotto. It is an Italian rice dish. However, since it is one of my absolute favorite dishes, I decided to "Southernize" it by adding a Southern favorite. Double the Southern Goodness.

Brown Sugar Acorn Squash

MAKES 2 SERVINGS

- 1 Acorn squash
- 4 Tbsp brown sugar
- 2 Tbsp butter, melted
- 1/4 Tsp salt

Cut squash in half lengthwise. Remove seeds. Arrange the squash halves, cut side down, in a 2-quart baking dish. Bake in a 350° oven for 45 minutes. Turn the squash halves cut side up.

In a small bowl, mix together brown sugar, butter and salt. Spoon brown sugar mixture into centers of squash halves. Bake for 20 to 25 minutes more or until squash is tender.

Collard Greens

MAKES 6-8 SERVINGS

- **1/2 Lb of smoked ham hocks**
- **2 Chicken bouillons**
- **1 Tbsp of hot sauce**
- **1 Tsp seasoning salt**
- **1 Tsp garlic salt**
- **1 Tbsp sugar**
- **Seasoning salt to taste**
- **1 Large bunch collard greens**

In a large stock pot add 4 quarts of water, smoked meat, chicken bouillon, hot sauce, seasoning salt, garlic salt and sugar. Simmer on medium heat and cook for 1 hour.

Wash collards thoroughly, checking each leaf for tiny bugs. Remove the stems that run down the center of the leaf. Stack about 5 leaves, roll and slice 1 inch thick. Wash again. Drain. Place greens in pot with meat and seasonings and cook about an hour or until tender. When tender, taste and add seasoning salt if needed.

NOTE: winter greens may only take 30 minutes to get tender, so check often.

TIPS:
I always keep Louisiana Hot Sauce® in my pantry. My favorite seasoning salt is Lawry's® brand, but you can use your favorite.

Collard greens are a staple at every holiday and family gathering in the South. There was not a family dinner without collard greens on the table. Many people have no idea that collards are a winter vegetable, which makes them taste much better at Thanksgiving and Christmas time. However, since they are the Southern food "anthem", we have them for every occasion, in any season. That's why it is so important that they are done right!

Fried Cajun Turkey Wings

MAKES 4 SERVINGS

- Fresh turkey wings, cooked
- 2 Eggs
- 1 Tbsp of cajun seasoning*
- 3 Cups flour
- 1 Quart of vegetable oil, for deep frying

Follow instructions for stewed turkey wings, on page 1except do not add flour at the end.

Mix eggs with 1/4 cup of water and beat well. Add to shallow pan. Mix together seasoning and flour. Add to shallow pan. Dip turkey wings into egg wash, then dip into seasoned flour and coat well.

Deep fry in oil for 7 minutes until golden brown. Remove and drain on paper towels. Enjoy!

Shown here with Cornbread Dressing and Cranberry Orange Sauce, see next page for recipes.

***TIP:**
There are several cajun seasoning types in the market. I prefer Slap Yo Mama Cajun Seasoning®.*

Cornbread Dressing

MAKES 6-8 SERVINGS

- Cornbread *(recipe below)*
- 10 Slices toasted white bread
- 1 Stick butter
- 1 Cup green bell peppers, chopped
- 1/2 Cup onion, small, diced
- 1/2 Cup celery
- 8 Cups turkey or chicken stock
- 1 Tsp poultry seasoning
- 1 Can cream of chicken soup

Preheat oven to 350°. In a large bowl, crumble cornbread and toasted bread. Set aside.

Melt butter in a large skillet over medium heat. Add bell pepper, onions and celery. Cook until onion is translucent (about 5 minutes). Pour vegetable mixture over cornbread mixture. Add stock, poultry seasoning and cream of chicken soup.

Taste mixture and add salt if needed. Pour mixture into a greased baking pan and bake until dressing is cooked through (about 45 minutes). *See photo on page 89.*

Cornbread for Dressing

Preheat oven to 350°. Combine all ingredients and mix well. Pour into a greased baking dish. Bake for 20–25 minutes.

1 Cup self-rising cornmeal
1 Box cornbread mix*
1/2 Cup self-rising flour
1 Can evaporated milk
3 Eggs
1 Cup water
1/4 Cup sugar
2 Tbsp vegetable oil

Cranberry Orange Sauce

MAKES 6-8 SERVINGS

- 2 Cups sugar
- 2 Cups water
- 4 Cups cranberries
- 2 Tsp grated orange zest
- Juice of 1 orange

Combine sugar and water, bring to a boil and stir until sugar is dissolved. Boil the syrup for 5 minutes. Add cranberries to the syrup and simmer uncovered.

Simmer without stirring for 5 minutes until berries pop and are translucent. Skim off any foam. Add orange zest and orange juice. Pour into glass dish and chill until set.

Red Beans and Rice

MAKES 8-10 SERVINGS

- 2 Lbs of red kidney beans
- 2 Cups of chopped onions
- 1/2 Cup green bell pepper
- 1/4 Cup red bell pepper
- 1 1/2 Cloves garlic, chopped
- 2 Tbsp chopped parsley
- 1 Lb of smoked ham, cubed
- 1 Lb of andouille sausage, sliced
- 1 Ham bone
- 1 Tbsp salt
- 1/2 Tsp black pepper
- 1/2 Tsp cayenne pepper
- 2 Bay leaves
- 2 Quarts water
- 4 Cups of white rice, cooked

In a large stockpot, cover beans with water and soak overnight in the refrigerator.

Add remaining ingredients, except rice. Cook on low for 3 hours. Stir often to make sure mixture does not stick. Remove bay leaves and serve beans over rice.

Okra and Tomatoes

MAKES 4 SERVINGS

- 4 Slices of bacon, chopped
- 1/2 Cup thinly sliced onion
- 1/4 Cup thinly sliced green bell pepper
- 15 1/2 Oz can chopped stewed tomatoes
- 1/2 Tsp salt
- 1/2 Tsp black pepper
- 1/2 Tsp sugar
- 10 Oz frozen cut okra

In a medium sauce pot, cook the bacon until crisp. Add onion and green pepper. Cook over medium heat for 5 minutes. Add tomatoes, salt, pepper and sugar.

Cook on medium for 10 minutes, stirring often to prevent sticking. Add okra and cook for 10 more minutes or until okra is tender. Taste and adjust seasoning as needed.

Creamed Corn

MAKES 4-6 SERVINGS

- 7 Ears fresh yellow corn
- 2 Tbsp butter
- 1 Tbsp flour
- 1 Cup heavy cream
- 1 Tbsp sugar
- Salt

Cut the corn kernels from the cob with a sharp knife. Using the back of the blade, scrape against the cob to remove the milky liquid.

In a large skillet, melt butter on medium heat. Add flour and stir. Cook for 3 minutes and whisk in cream. Bring to a simmer and stir in corn and sugar. Cook for 20 minutes and add salt to taste. Cook 5 minutes longer and serve hot.

Fried Cabbage

MAKES 4 SERVINGS

- 4 Strips of bacon, cut into pieces
- 1/4 Cup onions
- 1/4 Cup red bell peppers
- 4 Cubes chicken bouillon
- 1/4 Cup water
- 1 Tsp black pepper
- 1 Tsp accent
- 3 Tbsp sugar
- 1 Head of cabbage, chopped

Fry bacon until crispy. In the same pan, add onions and bell peppers and sauté until onions are translucent.

Add chicken bouillon, water, black pepper, accent and sugar. Dissolve bouillon and add cabbage. Simmer until cabbage is tender (about 10 to 15 minutes).

Field Peas

MAKES 4 SERVINGS

- **2 Lbs frozen field peas with snaps**
- **2 Chicken bouillon cubes**
- **2 Oz of pork jowls (cut in strips)**
- **Salt and pepper**

Bring 6 cups of water with bouillon cubes to a boil. Add peas and pork jowls. Bring to a boil, cover and reduce heat. Simmer for 45 to 60 minutes, stirring often to make sure peas do not stick.

Add small amounts of water if peas become too dry. Once peas are tender, add salt and pepper to your desired taste.

Sweet Potato Casserole

MAKES 8-10 SERVINGS

- 4 Cups sweet potatoes (about 2 pounds)
- 1/2 Cup white sugar
- 2 Eggs
- 1/2 Tsp salt
- 4 Tbsp butter, softened
- 2 Tbsp all purpose flour
- 1/2 Cup evaporated milk
- 1/4 Tsp nutmeg
- 1/2 Tsp vanilla extract
- 1 Tsp lemon extract

PECAN TOPPING:

- 1/2 Cup packed brown sugar
- 1/3 Cup all purpose flour
- 3 Tbsp butter, softened
- 1/2 Cup chopped pecans
- Mini marshmallows (optional)

Preheat oven to 325°. Cut off each end of sweet potatoes and boil until tender. Peel, drain and beat with a mixer.

In a large bowl, mix together the sweet potatoes, sugar, eggs, salt, butter, flour, milk, nutmeg, and extracts. Mix until smooth. Transfer to a 9 x 13 inch baking dish.

In medium bowl, mix the brown sugar and flour. Cut in the butter until the mixture is course. Stir in the pecans. Sprinkle the mixture over the sweet potato mixture.

Bake in the preheated oven 30 minutes, or until the topping is lightly brown. Sprinkle with marshmallows if desired and bake five minutes longer.

Braised Beef Short Ribs

MAKES 4 SERVINGS

- 5 Lbs of thick cut, lean, beef short ribs
- 1/4 Cup vegetable oil
- 1 1/2 Cup flour
- 2 Tsp seasoned salt
- 1 Tsp black pepper
- 1 Tsp garlic powder
- 1 Cup onions
- 1 Cup of mushrooms
- 1 Cup red wine (cabernet sauvignon or merlot)
- 1 Cup water
- 1 Bay leaf
- 2 Tbsp flour
- 1/4 Cup water
- Salt and pepper

Heat oil in a dutch oven on medium high heat, season the ribs with seasoned salt, pepper and garlic. Dredge ribs in flour. Brown ribs on all sides in oil. When done, add onions and mushrooms and sauté lightly. Add water, wine and bay leaf. Cover tightly and transfer to the oven and cook at 325° for two hours.

Remove ribs and bay leaf from dutch oven. Mix flour with water and add to dutch oven and cook for 5 minutes until sauce thickens. Season sauce with salt and pepper and add short ribs back to the dutch oven.

Yukon Gold Mashed Potatoes

MAKES 8-10 SERVINGS

- 4 Lbs Yukon Gold potatoes, peeled and cut into large chunks
- 10 Oz heavy cream
- 6 Oz butter
- 1 Tbsp kosher salt

Place cut potatoes in large pot and cover with salted cold water. Bring to a slight boil. Boil until potatoes are fork tender, about 30 minutes.

While potatoes are cooking, place butter and cream in a separate small saucepan and heat over low heat until butter is melted and milk is hot (but not boiling).

Drain potatoes while hot and pass through a food mill or a potato ricer. Put back into the hot pot that they were cooked in.

Slowly pour in the warm butter and cream mixture and incorporate gently. Taste and adjust seasoning as needed.

Barbecue Pigs Feet

MAKES 4 SERVINGS

- **4 Pigs feet, split in half lengthwise**
- **2 Cups onion, sliced**
- **2 Tbsp salt**
- **1/4 Cup vinegar**
- **2 Tbsp hot sauce**
- **2 Cups barbecue sauce**

Wash pigs feet very well, removing any hair by scraping with a sharp knife.

Place the first five ingredients in a large pot and cover with water. Bring water to a boil over medium high heat and then reduce heat to a medium simmer. Simmer for 2 1/2 hours.

Remove pigs feet from the cooking broth. Place the meat in a roasting pan and cover with barbecue sauce. Bake tightly covered with foil in a 325° oven for 30 minutes. Uncover and bake for an additional 20 minutes.

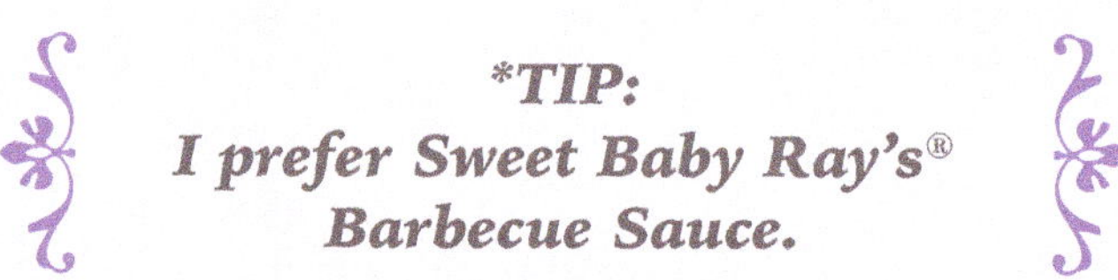

***TIP:**
I prefer Sweet Baby Ray's® Barbecue Sauce.

Black Pepper Crusted Prime Rib

MAKES 4 SERVINGS

- 1 Prime rib roast (large, 8 lbs and up)
- 1/4 Cup vegetable oil
- 2 Tbsp coarsely ground black pepper
- 2 Tbsp kosher salt
- 2 Tbsp garlic cloves, finely chopped
- 2 Tbsp spicy brown mustard*

Preheat oven to 450°. Combine all ingredients (except the roast) in a medium bowl. Rub roast with mixture and place roast, fat side up, in a shallow roasting pan. Bake uncovered for 15 minutes.

Reduce heat to 325°. Bake for 2 hours or until meat reaches desired doneness (for medium rare, 145°; medium, 150°; well, 165°), basting with drippings every 30 minutes.

Let roast stand for 20 minutes before slicing. Serve with horseradish sauce *(see recipe below)*.

TIPS:
I prefer Gulden's® Spicy Brown Mustard and Grey Poupon® Dijon Mustard.

Horseradish Sauce

MAKES 4 SERVINGS

- 3 Tbsp of prepared horseradish
- 1/4 Cup sour cream
- 1 Tbsp mayonnaise
- 1 Tbsp lemon juice (fresh)
- 1/4 Tsp salt
- 1/4 Tsp pepper

Mix all ingredients together until well combined.

Best Ever Rib Eye Steaks

MAKES 2 SERVINGS

- 2 – 12 to 16 oz boneless rib eye steaks
- 1/2 Stick butter, softened
- 1 Tsp minced garlic
- 1 Tbsp of lemon juice (fresh)
- 1 Tbsp of worcestershire sauce
- Kosher salt
- Fresh ground pepper
- Vegetable oil

Let steaks come to room temperature for about 30 minutes. Meanwhile, in a small bowl, mix together butter, garlic, lemon juice, and worcestershire sauce.

In a large cast iron skillet, heat oil over high heat. Season steaks with a generous amount of salt and pepper. Add steaks to skillet and cook for about 5 minutes then turn steaks over and cook for about 3 minutes.

Add butter mixture to skillet, and with a large spoon baste steaks, spooning butter over steaks several times. Cook for a few more minutes. Transfer steaks to a plate and cover with foil. Let rest for 10 minutes. (Steaks should be medium rare).

Chicken Spaghetti

MAKES 8-10 SERVINGS

- 1 Whole chicken, boiled
- 1 Can cream of mushroom soup (10 3/4 oz)
- 1 Stick of butter, melted
- 1 Tsp paprika
- 8 Oz sharp cheddar cheese, shredded
- 8 Oz spaghetti noodles

Cook spaghetti pasta in chicken broth from whole boiled chicken, adding water if necessary. Cook al dente and drain.

Mix chopped up chicken with soup, butter, paprika and half of cheese. Add the mixture to a casserole dish and top with cheese. Bake at 350° for 30 minutes.

Chitterlings

MAKES 6-8 SERVINGS

- 10 Lbs chitterlings
- 1/4 Cup apple cider vinegar (for cleaning in first boil)
- 1 Green pepper, chopped
- 1/2 Onion, chopped
- 3 Stalks of celery, chopped
- 2 Tbsp seasoning salt
- 1 Tbsp of black pepper
- 1 Tsp of granulated garlic
- 3 Tbsp of hot sauce
- 3 Tbsp of apple cider vinegar

Clean chitterlings thoroughly, by removing any fat, debris or anything that looks like crumbs. It takes about one hour per 10 pounds, because you must go over each piece. Combine chitterlings and vinegar in a large stock pot and cover with water. Bring to a slow boil about 7 minutes, then drain and rinse.

Add chitterlings, green pepper, onion, celery, seasoning salt, black pepper, granulated garlic, hot sauce, and vinegar to a large stock pot. Cover with water and bring to a low boil. Cover with lid and cook for three hours until chitterlings are tender. Checking and stirring from the bottom often to make sure they are not sticking. Add more water if needed. Adjust seasonings to your taste and serve hot over white rice.

Chit'lins

The correct word is chitterlings, but if you say chitterlings that means you did not grow up eating them. And if you didn't grow up eating them, there's a strong possibility that you won't like them. They are only prepared during the holidays because of the amount of time it takes to clean them thoroughly (they're pig intestines). It's a known fact that you either love them or hate them. But more and more people are learning to love them, as they have become a delicacy in many upscale restaurants.

Vidalia Onion Pie

MAKES 6-8 SERVINGS

- 3 Cups onions, thinly sliced
- 3 Tbsp butter
- Pastry shell, baked
- 1/2 Cup whole milk
- 1 1/2 Cup sour cream
- 2 Eggs
- 2 Tbsp flour
- 1 1/2 Tsp salt
- 4 Slices bacon, cooked crispy and chopped

Sauté onions in butter, spoon onions into pastry shell and mix milk with sour cream and eggs. Sift flour and salt together. Add dry ingredients with wet ingredients. Add to pastry shell and bake on 325° for 30 minutes. Garnish with bacon pieces.

Chicken Fried Cubed Steak

MAKES 2-4 SERVINGS

- 4 Cubed steaks
- 1 Cup self-rising flour
- 1 Tsp seasoned salt
- 1 Tsp garlic powder
- 1 Tsp black pepper
- 1/2 Cup vegetable oil

Mix the flour, seasoned salt, garlic and pepper in a bowl. Coat both sides of cubed steak with mixture. Heat oil in a frying pan over medium high heat and brown steaks well on both sides. Remove steak and drain on paper towels. Drain oil leaving 2 tbsp at the bottom of the frying pan for the chicken fried steak gravy below.

Chicken Fried Steak Gravy

- 2 Tbsp of reserved oil
- 1/2 Onion, sliced thin
- 1/4 Cup green bell pepper
- 1 Tbsp of reserved seasoned flour from above mixture
- 1 1/2 Cup water
- 1/4 Tsp browning and seasoning sauce*
- Salt and pepper

Add onions and peppers to frying pan. Sauté until onions are translucent. Add flour and stir for one minute. Add water and whisk well. Add a browning and seasoning sauce and simmer until thick. Season gravy with salt and pepper, return steaks to pan and serve.

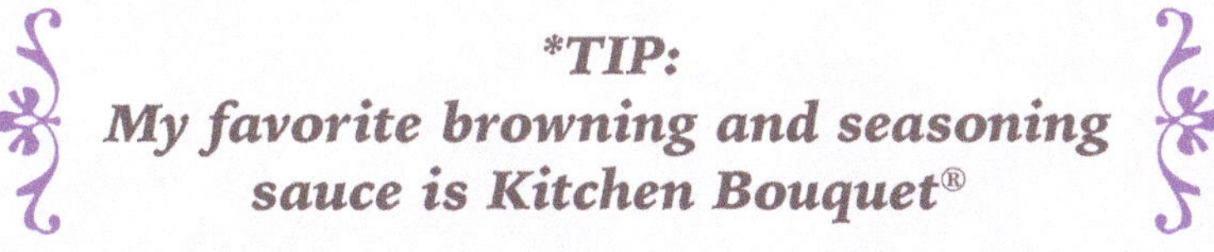

Fried Gizzards

MAKES 4 SERVINGS

- 1 Lb chicken gizzards, rinsed
- 1 Tbsp of salt
- 3 Tbsp of apple cider vinegar
- 3 Cups vegetable oil
- 1 Cup of flour
- 1 Tsp seasoning salt
- 1 Tsp black pepper
- 1/2 Tsp granulated garlic
- 1 Tsp paprika
- 1 Egg

Place gizzards in a medium sized stock pot and add salt and vinegar, cover gizzards with water. Bring to a slow boil, cover and cook for one hour, until gizzards are tender. Drain gizzards from cooking liquid and set aside.

Heat frying oil to 350°, in a small bowl add egg with 3 tablespoons of water and whisk together. Combine flour, seasoning salt, black pepper, granulated garlic, and paprika to a plastic zip bag. Shake flour mixture together.

Dip gizzards in egg mixture and then add gizzards to the bag of flour mixture and tightly close, shake well. Remove gizzards from the flour mixture, shaking off excess flour and add to hot oil. Fry for 5 to 7 minutes until golden brown. Drain the gizzards on paper towels, serve hot with your favorite hot sauce.

Fried Pork Chops

MAKES 3-5 SERVINGS

- 5 Center-cut pork chops
- 1 1/2 Cups flour
- 1 Tsp seasoned salt
- 1 Tsp black pepper
- 1 Tsp garlic powder
- 1 Tsp paprika
- 1 Cup vegetable oil

Combine flour with seasoned salt, black pepper, garlic powder, and paprika. Moisten pork chops with water and dredge in seasoned flour mixture. Fry on both sides for about 4 minutes each. Remove from oil and drain on paper towels.

Smothered Pork Chops

MAKES 3-5 SERVINGS

- Fry pork chops using recipe above.
- 1/2 Onion
- 2 Tbsp leftover seasoned flour
- 2 Cups hot water

Reserve 2 tbsp. Oil in frying pan and add onions and sauté until tender and add flour. Whisk for one minute on medium heat. Whisk in hot water and simmer. Add chops and simmer for 5 minutes.

Herb Roasted Chicken

MAKES 4-6 SERVINGS

- 1 Chicken, 4 to 6 lbs.
- 1/2 Stick butter, softened
- 1 Tbsp garlic
- 1 Tsp paprika
- 1 Tbsp seasoned salt
- 1 Sprig of thyme
- 1 Sprig of rosemary

Preheat the oven to 350°. Rub chicken with butter, season with garlic, paprika and seasoning salt. Place the thyme and rosemary in the cavity of the chicken. Place chicken in a roasting pan and cook uncovered for 55 minutes. Check with an internal thermometer until the temperature reaches 165°, testing the thigh part of the chicken which takes the longest to cook.

Try serving this dish with our Roasted Root Vegetable recipe below.

Roasted Root Vegetables

MAKES 6 SERVINGS

- 3 Cups parsnips
- 3 Cups carrots
- 3 Cups rutabaga
- 1 Tbsp olive oil
- 2 Tbsp sugar
- 1/2 Tsp salt
- 1/2 Tsp ground pepper

Preheat oven to 400°.

Toss vegetables, olive oil, sugar, salt and pepper. Spread on a baking sheet and roast until tender and golden brown—about 45 minutes.

Hoppin' John

MAKES 6-8 SERVINGS

- 1 1 Ham hock
- 2 Lbs of frozen black-eyed peas
- 1 Cup finely chopped onion
- 1 Tsp garlic
- 1 Tsp black pepper
- 1 Tsp salt
- 1 Cup rice, uncooked

Put enough water in pot to cover ham hock. Bring to a boil. Turn the heat to low and cook slowly until tender – about 1 hour. Remove ham hock and add water to make 4 cups liquid. Put the liquid back into the pot and add the peas, onions, garlic, pepper, and salt. Bring to a boil. Add rice. Stir well and cover. Reduce heat to low and simmer for 30 minutes. Meanwhile chop meat off of ham hock and add it back to pot.

Lemon Rosemary Rack of Lamb

MAKES 4 SERVINGS

- 2 Racks of lamb, frenched (1 1/2 lbs each rack)
- 4 Garlic cloves, minced
- 1 Tbsp fresh rosemary leaves, chopped
- 1 Tbsp lemon zest
- 2 Tbsp lemon juice
- 2 Tsp kosher salt
- 1 Tsp paprika
- 1 Tsp fresh ground pepper
- 1/4 Cup vegetable oil

Mix all ingredients except lamb in a large bowl. Add lamb racks, tossing to coat. Let marinate for 1 hour at room temperature. Preheat oven to 400°.

Transfer lamb to a roasting pan. Roast in oven for 20 minutes or until 140° (medium) or desired doneness. Let rest for 10 minutes before serving.

When I want to be fancy-dancy, I rely on my formal training to make "foo-foo" food for my family and clients. Lemon rosemary rack of lamb is one of those dishes that I make to get in touch with my classical side. And, since I've discovered that it is a favorite of my first lady, Lady Narlene McLaughlin, I have the opportunity to make it more frequently.

No one can resist the stickiness of oxtails when they are cooked perfectly. The natural gelatinous juices that come from the bones help to enhance the flavor. Try as you may to eat properly using a fork and knife. However, you won't be able to resist picking them up with your hands while trying to reach every nook and cranny of juicy goodness. Talk about tender love.

Slow Braised Oxtails

MAKES 4 SERVINGS

- 6 Lbs oxtails
- Salt and pepper
- 1/2 Cup flour
- 1/4 Cup oil
- 1/2 Cup diced green peppers
- 1 Cup onions
- 1 Cup red wine
- Water
- 1 Tsp garlic powder
- 1 Tsp seasoned salt*
- 1 Tsp black pepper

Season oxtails with salt and pepper, dredge oxtails in flour and brown in oil in a large pot. Remove oxtails. Add peppers and onions. Sauté until translucent add red wine and reduce for 5 minutes.

Return oxtails to the pot. Cover oxtails with water and add remaining seasonings. Cook on medium heat until tender, takes about 3 hours. Check often and add small amounts of water if necessary.

***TIP:**
I prefer Lawry's® Seasoned Salt.

Smoked Sausage with Tomatoes and Corn

MAKES 4-6 SERVINGS

- 1 Package smoked beef sausage, cut into 1 inch slices
- 2 Tbsp vegetable oil
- 1/2 Bell pepper, cut into strips
- 1/2 Onion, thinly sliced
- 28 Oz can diced tomatoes
- 1 Tbsp fresh rosemary, finely chopped
- 1 Lb bag frozen corn
- 1 Tsp garlic
- 1 Tsp sugar
- 1 Tsp seasoning salt
- Salt and pepper (to taste)

Sauté sausage in a large frying pan with oil, browning on both sides. Add bell peppers and onions and cook until onions are translucent.

Add tomatoes, rosemary, corn, garlic, sugar, seasoning salt and cook for an additional 20–25 minutes on medium low heat. Taste and add salt and pepper to your taste. Serve over rice.

Turkey Whole Grain Spaghetti

MAKES 4 SERVINGS

- 1 Lb ground turkey
- 6 Oz smoked turkey sausage, sliced on bias
- 1 Tsp seasoning salt
- 1/2 Tsp garlic powder
- 1/2 Tsp black pepper
- 1 Cup mushrooms, sliced
- 1/2 Cup onions, chopped
- 1/4 Cup bell peppers, chopped
- 2 Lb 13 oz spaghetti sauce
- 13.25 Oz whole grain spaghetti
- 2–3 Tbsp of parmesan cheese

Add seasonings to ground turkey and brown in large skillet. Add sliced turkey sausage. Cook until browned. Add mushrooms, onions and bell pepper. Cook until onions are translucent. Add spaghetti sauce and simmer for 15 minutes on medium low heat.

Cook pasta according to package directions. Serve the pasta with spaghetti sauce then sprinkle with fresh, grated parmesan cheese.

Seafood Mac and Cheese

MAKES 8-10 SERVINGS

- **Mac and cheese**
- **1/2 Lb shrimp**
- **1 Tsp seafood seasoning spices***
- **1 Tbsp butter**
- **1/2 Lb claw crab meat, picked over for shells**
- **1 Tsp yellow mustard**
- **1/2 Cup mozzarella cheese, shredded**

Start with Mac and Cheese recipe, (from page 82) uncooked, replace the cheddar cheese for topping with mozzarella cheese.

Heat oven to 325°.

Sauté shrimp in seafood seasoning and butter. Remove shrimp from pan and discard any juices left in pan. Add shrimp, crabmeat and mustard to mac and cheese mixture.

Stir well and put into a baking dish and top with mozzarella cheese. Cook in oven for 45 minutes uncovered until golden brown.

Cookout at My House

Southern Baked Beans

MAKES 8 SERVINGS

- 2 – 16 Oz cans of pork and beans
- 1/2 Cup dark brown sugar
- 1/4 Cup of hickory barbecue sauce
- 1/2 Green bell pepper, diced small
- 4 Bacon strips

Preheat oven to 325°.

In a baking dish, combine pork and beans, brown sugar, barbecue sauce, and bell pepper. Top with bacon strips. Bake uncovered for 30 to 45 minutes.

Cole Slaw

MAKES 8 SERVINGS

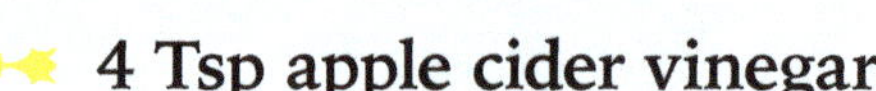

- 4 Tsp apple cider vinegar
- 4 Tbsp vegetable oil
- 1/2 Cup chopped onion
- 3 Cups sandwich spread*
- 1 Tsp celery salt
- 1 Cup sugar
- 2 Carrots, grated
- 2 Heads cabbage, grated

Mix together vinegar, oil, onion, sandwich spread, celery salt, and sugar. Pour over carrots and cabbage. Fold well. Refrigerate overnight for best results.

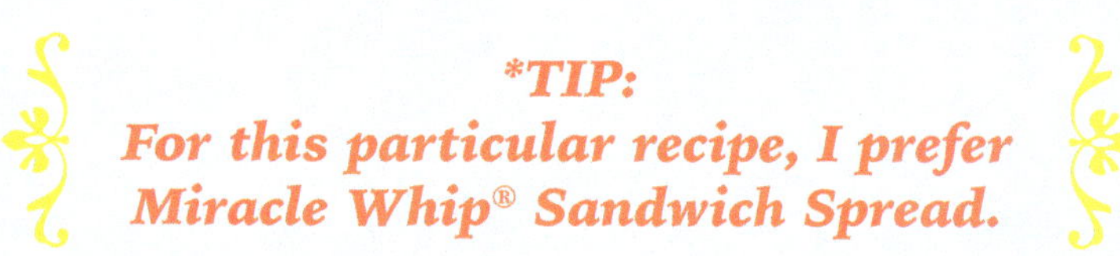

TIP:
For this particular recipe, I prefer Miracle Whip® Sandwich Spread.

Broccoli Salad

MAKES 6-8 SERVINGS

- 2 Bunches broccoli florets, cut in small pieces
- 1/2 Cup raisins
- 10 To 12 slices bacon, fried and crumbled
- 1/2 Cup shredded cheddar cheese

Combine broccoli, raisins, bacon and cheese.

Dressing

- 1 Cup mayonnaise
- 2 Tbsp red wine vinegar
- 2 Tsp sugar

Combine mayonnaise, vinegar, and sugar.

Pour dressing over broccoli salad mixture and marinate in refrigerator for 1 to 2 hours.

Citrus Vinaigrette

MAKES 4 SERVINGS

- 2 Tbsp fresh squeezed orange juice
- 2 Tbsp lemon or lime juice
- 1 Tsp Dijon style mustard*
- 2 Tbsp honey
- 1/4 Cup olive oil
- Dash of salt and pepper to taste

Combine all ingredients except olive oil. Whisk together, then slowly drizzle in olive oil, whisking to combine.

This citrus vinaigrette is great over a summer salad or even your favorite grilled fish.

TIP:
I prefer Grey Poupon Dijon® Mustard.

Cucumbers, Tomatoes and Onions

MAKES 4-6 SERVINGS

- 2 Med purple onions
- 2 Cucumbers
- 3 Fresh tomatoes chopped
- 1 Tsp salt
- Black pepper to taste
- 1/4 Cup vinegar

Slice the onions and cucumbers and dice the tomatoes. Mix together in a bowl. Add salt, pepper and vinegar. Marinate for 1 hour in refrigerator and serve.

Pickled Okra

MAKES 8 SERVINGS

- 1 1/2 Lbs of fresh okra
- 4 Garlic cloves
- 2 Cups apple cider vinegar
- 2 Cups water
- 3 Tbsp kosher salt
- 1 Tbsp sugar

PICKLING SPICES

- 2 Tbsp mustard seeds
- 1 Tbsp red pepper flakes
- 1 Tsp black peppercorns
- 4 – 1 Pint canning jars

Prepare for canning by sterilizing jars and lids. Place garlic, vinegar, water, salt and sugar in a medium saucepan. Bring to a boil to dissolve the salt and sugar. Reduce heat and keep warm. Pack okra in the jars along with pickling spices.

Pour warm vinegar mixture into the jars, up to 1/4 inch from the rim of the jars. Run a knife between the okra and the jars to release any air bubbles. Place sterilized lids on jars. Follow standard sterilized rules. Let sit 24 hours before eating.

Potato Salad

MAKES 6-8 SERVINGS

- 2 Lbs red bliss potatoes
- 1 Tbsp salt for boiling water
- 1 1/2 Cup mayonnaise*
- 2 Tbsp yellow mustard
- 2 Tsp seasoning salt
- 2 Tsp sugar
- 1/4 Tsp cayenne pepper
- 1 Tsp Spanish paprika
- 1/4 Cup red bell pepper, chopped fine
- 1/4 Cup celery, chopped fine
- 4 Hard boiled eggs, peeled and chopped

Peel and cut 5 to 6 medium red bliss potatoes into 3/4 inch cubes. Cover potatoes with salted water in 4 quart saucepot. Bring to a boil over medium – high heat. Reduce heat to low and simmer until potatoes are tender (about 10 minutes). Drain and cool.

Combine mayonnaise, mustard, seasoning salt, sugar, cayenne pepper and paprika. Add bell peppers, celery, eggs and potatoes. Mix well. Refrigerate for several hours before serving.

***TIP:**
For this particular recipe, I prefer Hellman's® Mayonnaise.

Sweet and Spicy Pickles

MAKES 10 SERVINGS

- 3 Lbs pickling cucumbers, sliced into 1/4 inch slices
- 1 Medium onion, sliced
- 1/2 Cup pickling salt
- 6 Cups water
- 3 Cups white vinegar
- 1 1/2 Cups apple cider vinegar
- 3 Cups sugar
- 2 Tbsp mustard seeds
- 1/2 Tbsp whole black peppercorns
- 7 Cloves garlic
- 2 Tsp crushed red pepper flakes

Place cucumbers, onions, pickling salt and water in a large plastic bowl. Cover and allow cucumbers to soak for 2 hours. Drain water from the onions and cucumbers and rinse well to remove salt. Drain well and set aside.

Combine the vinegars, sugar, mustard seeds, peppercorns, garlic and pepper flakes in a medium saucepan over high heat. Bring to a boil, reduce heat to medium and add the cucumbers and onions. Bring to a simmer for 5 minutes then remove from heat.

Let pickles cool. Add to mason jars and refrigerate for 1 week before using. Keep refrigerated.

Seafood Pasta Salad

MAKES 6-8 SERVINGS

- 8 Oz rotini pasta
- 1/4 Cup red bell peppers, chopped small
- 2 Stalks celery, chopped small
- 1/2 Lb of cooked shrimp, peeled and deveined
- 1/2 Lb imitation crabmeat
- 1 Can tuna fish, drained
- 1 1/2 Cups mayonnaise
- 1 Tbsp seafood seasoning spices*
- 1/2 Tsp cayenne pepper
- 1 Tbsp yellow mustard

Bring a large pot of lightly salted water to a boil. Add pasta and cook for 8 to 10 minutes until al dente; rinse under cold water until cool, then drain.

In a large bowl add all ingredients and stir to combine well. Adjust mayo and seasonings to your taste. Refrigerate for several hours before serving.

***TIP:**
I prefer Old Bay® Seasoning for Seafood Seasoning Spices.

Garlic Blue Crabs

MAKES 2-4 SERVINGS

- 1 Dozen cooked blue crabs (see the recipe on page 140)
- 1/2 Lb butter, melted
- 2 Tbsp granulated garlic (divided)
- 2 Tbsp hot sauce
- 2 Tsp cajun seasoning (divided)

Clean outer shell of crabs, leaving legs and body of crab intact. Combine melted butter, 1 tablespoon garlic, hot sauce, and 1 teaspoon of cajun seasoning together.

Sprinkle remaining garlic and cajun seasoning on crabs, then pour butter mixture on top of crabs. Enjoy.

DUUUUU-VAAAAAL! Garlic crabs are an original favorite of Duval County. The very first restaurant that I opened specialized in garlic crabs and shrimp. At that time, you could only find two or three other places that served garlic crabs. Today, there is a "crab house" on every corner.

Grilled Oysters

MAKES 4 SERVINGS

- 36 Oysters, shucked and on the half shell
- 2 Sticks butter
- 1 Whole garlic bulb, peeled and finely chopped
- Juice of 1 lemon
- 1 Tbsp worcestershire sauce
- 2 Tbsp cajun seasoning
- 2 Oz white wine (chardonnay, chablis, etc)
- 2 Sticks of butter, cubed
- 8 Oz grated parmesan cheese

SAUCE: In a saucepan bring 2 sticks of butter to a simmer. Add garlic, lemon juice, worcestershire sauce and cajun seasoning. Cook for 2 minutes and add white wine. Remove from heat and let cool for 4 minutes.

In a separate bowl, combine the remaining butter cut into cubes to the garlic mixture. Stir sauce until the butter is melted and combined with garlic mixture.

Preheat grill to 350°. Place oysters on the grill and add a tablespoon of sauce to each oyster, doing them in small batches. Add cheese and allow cheese to melt. Serve immediately.

***TIP:**
I prefer Slap Yo Mama® Cajun Seasoning.

I was so impressed with the grilled oysters I had at a restaurant that I decided to try making them myself. With a bit of my own twist, I was able to develop a recipe that fastly became a family and client favorite. More than a party pleaser, I would bet that anyone who thinks they don't like oysters would change their story if they tried these. Uber delicious!

Hot Souse or Pork Pot

MAKES 8-10 SERVINGS

- 4 Pig feet, split
- 4 Pig ears
- 4 Pig tails
- 1 Onion
- 1 Green bell pepper
- 1/4 Cup vinegar
- 2 Tbsp red pepper flakes
- 2 Tbsp seasoning salt
- 1 Tsp black pepper
- 1 Tsp granulated garlic
- 1 Large can diced tomatoes
- Water

Wash pig feet, pig ears and pig tails well. Remove any hairs with a sharp knife. In a large stock pot add pig parts, onion, bell pepper, vinegar and seasonings. Add water to cover.

Bring to a boil, reduce heat and simmer until meat is tender and falling off the bones (about 2 hours). Remove as many large bones as possible, then add tomatoes and cook for 30 minutes. Adjust seasonings to suit your taste. Serve hot with crackers or cornbread. *See our cornbread recipe on page 74.*

Moscato Spicy Garlic Shrimp

MAKES 4 SERVINGS

- 1 1/2 Lb jumbo shrimp, shelled and deveined
- 1 Tsp seafood seasoning spices*
- 1 Tsp granulated garlic
- 1/2 Tsp cayenne pepper
- 2 Tbsp butter
- 1/4 Cup moscato wine
- 1 Tbsp freshly squeezed lemon juice
- 1 Tbsp butter (additional)

Season shrimp with old bay, garlic and cayenne pepper. Add butter to a large skillet and add seasoned shrimp. Cook shrimp for 2 minutes on both sides. Transfer shrimp to a bowl.

Return pan back to heat and add moscato and lemon juice. Boil the liquid until it is slightly thickened about 30 seconds. Add butter and allow to melt, then pour sauce over shrimp.

*TIP:
I prefer Old Bay® Seasoning for Seafood Seasoning Spices.

Pan Fried Whiting

MAKES 4 SERVINGS

- **2 Lbs of whiting (pan fried split, 3–4 fish)**
- **1/4 Cup hot sauce***
- **1 1/2 Cup cornmeal**
- **1/2 Cup flour**
- **1 Tsp lemon pepper**
- **1/4 Tsp seasoning salt**
- **3 Cups vegetable oil for deep frying**

In a shallow pan, pour hot sauce over whiting.

In a large bowl, combine cornmeal, flour and seasonings. Mix well. Heat oil to 350° in a large skillet. Add fish to cornmeal mixture, coating well. Fry fish until golden brown, about 4 minutes on each side, making sure not to overcrowd pan so fish can lay flat.

***TIP:**
I prefer Louisiana Hot Sauce®.

Pan Fried Catfish Nuggets

MAKES 4 SERVINGS

- 1 Lb catfish nuggets
- 1 Beaten egg
- 3 Tbsp hot sauce*
- 2/3 Cup cornmeal
- 1/4 Cup flour
- 1 Tsp seasoning salt
- 1/4 Tsp black pepper
- Vegetable oil for frying

Rinse fish and pat dry with paper towels. In a shallow dish, combine egg and hot sauce. In another dish, stir together cornmeal, flour, seasoning salt and black pepper. Dip fish in egg mixture; coat fish with corn meal mixture. Set aside.

In a large skillet, heat 1/4 inch of oil. Add half of the fish in a single layer, frying on one side until golden brown. Turn and fry on second side until golden brown.

Check the thicker pieces and make sure they flake in the center. (Catfish can take longer than other fish 5 to 6 minutes per side). Drain on paper towels. Keep warm in oven set at 250° while frying the remainder of the fish.

Slow Boil Blue Crabs

MAKES 8-10 SERVINGS

- 3 Dozen live blue crabs
- 3 Onions, quartered
- 1 Whole celery, chopped large
- 4 Lemons, quartered
- 1/2 Cup kosher salt
- 1/2 Cup granulated garlic
- 2 – 12 Oz cans of beer
- 5 Lb bag red bliss potatoes
- 16 Corn cobbettes
- 4 Lbs smoked sausage, cut in thirds
- 4 1/2 Lb bag seafood seasoning*

Fill a 42 quart stock pot fitted with a steamer basket. Fill about 1/3 full with water. Bring to a boil. Add onions, celery, lemons, salt, garlic and beer. Bring to a boil, then add potatoes, corn, and sausage.

Allow to boil for 15 minutes. Add crab and shrimp boil seasoning and crabs. Boil for 20 minutes. Turn off heat and let sit for 15 minutes. Remove basket from pot and dump out on a table lined with newspapers and enjoy!

***TIP:**
My preference is the Louisiana Crab and Shrimp Boil Seasoning® mix. I keep it stocked in my pantry!

Varon's Grilled Pork Ribs

MAKES 8-10 SERVINGS

- 2 Slabs pork ribs
- 1 Tbsp lemon pepper seasoning
- 1 Tbsp seasoning salt
- 1 Tsp granulated garlic
- 1 Tbsp paprika
- 2 Tbsp brown sugar
- 1 Tsp cayenne pepper
- 1 Cup apple cider vinegar, divided
- 2 Cups water
- Spray bottle

Clean excess fat from ribs. Combine seasonings and brown sugar together. Rub ribs with seasoning, leaving some seasoning for later use.

Preheat grill to medium low heat (about 300°). Place ribs on grill. In spray bottle, add 1 teaspoon of seasoning, 1/2 cup apple cider vinegar, 1 cup of water. Shake bottle.

Spray ribs every 20 minutes with vinegar mixture. Cook ribs for about 1 1/2 hours. Once ribs are done, combine the rest of the vinegar mixture. Add ribs to roasting pan and add liquid vinegar mixture. Cover with foil and allow to steam on grill for 30 additional minutes. Let rest for 15 minutes before cutting.

They say a way to a man's heart is through his stomach. I say a way to a woman's heart is through her man cooking meat on the grill. When my husband takes his time (and I don't make him mad trying to tell him what to do), his ribs cannot be beat. Don't leave out steaming them in the extra marinade – that makes them extra, extra tender. Ladies, be sure to let him know just how much you appreciate his tenderness.

A Family Favorite

Pistachio Salad

MAKES 6-8 SERVINGS

- **1 Box instant pistachio pudding**
- **1 10 Oz can crushed pineapple, not drained**
- **9 Oz frozen whipped topping***
- **1/2 Package miniature marshmallows**
- **1/2 Cup chopped pistachios**

Mix pudding and pineapple together, add cool whip and mix. Mix in marshmallows and nuts. Place in 9 x 9 inch or 8 x 12 inch pan and place in refrigerator for 2 to 3 hours, or overnight.

***TIP:**
I prefer Cool Whip® frozen whipped topping.

Lemon Pepper Chicken Wings

MAKES 2-4 SERVINGS

- 2 Lbs of chicken wings
- 1/4 Cup hot sauce*
- 1/4 Cup butter
- 1 Tbsp lemon pepper seasoning
- 1 Tbsp fresh lemon juice
- 1/4 Tsp salt
- 1/4 Tsp black pepper
- Vegetable oil for frying

Microwave hot sauce, butter, and lemon pepper seasoning for 1 minute or until sauce is creamy when stirred. Add lemon juice and stir. Set sauce aside. Season wings with salt and black pepper. Fry wings in oil that is heated to 350° for 15 minutes.

Drain cooked wings on paper towels and toss in sauce until coated. Serve wings with bleu cheese dressing and celery sticks.

For my bleu cheese dressing, go to page 15.

Honey Drippers

MAKES 6 SERVINGS

- 1 – 46 Oz can pineapple juice
- 2 Cups sugar
- 1 – 8 Oz Can crushed pineapple
- 6 – 12 Oz cups

In a large pitcher, add pineapple juice. Stir in sugar and crushed pineapple with juice. Stir until sugar is dissolved. Add juice to cups and put into freezer until frozen solid.

Golden Pound Cake
with Grilled Pineapple and Caramel Rum Sauce

MAKES 12-16 SERVINGS

- Golden pound cake
- 3 Sticks of salted butter
- 1 Cup of sour cream
- 3 Cups sugar
- 6 Eggs
- 3 Cups cake flour
- 1 Tsp vanilla flavor
- 1 Tsp lemon flavor

Cream butter, sour cream and sugar. Add eggs, 1 at a time, then flavorings, mixing the entire time. (Batter should be fluffy). Gradually add flour. Mix on medium until smooth, about 2 minutes. Bake at 325° f for about 1 1/2 hours, checking after 1 hour.

Grilled Pineapple

- Pineapple (cut into 1/2 inch circles)
- Canola oil

Brush the pineapple on both sides with the oil and place on the grill. Grill until golden brown and caramelized on both sides, about 2 to 4 minutes on each side. Cut into big chunks.

Caramel Rum Sauce

- 1 Cup heavy cream
- 1 Cup packed dark brown sugar
- 4 Tbsp salted butter
- 3 Tbsp rum

Combine the cream, brown sugar, and butter in a medium saucepan. Bring to a boil and then reduce heat to low and simmer for 5 minutes. Stir in rum. Top each piece of pound cake with some of the pineapple and a scoop of vanilla ice cream. Drizzle with the caramel rum sauce.

Georgia Peach Ice Cream

MAKES 4 SERVINGS

- 4 Cups half and half
- 1 1/2 Cups sugar
- 1 Tbsp vanilla
- 2 Cups heavy whipping cream
- 4 Cups Georgia peaches, peeled and seeded

In a large bowl combine half and half, sugar, and vanilla. Stir until sugar dissolves. Stir in whipping cream. In a blender, blend peaches until nearly smooth. Stir fruit into ice cream mixture.

Freeze ice cream mixture in a 5 quart ice cream maker according to the manufacturer's directions. Put into freezer for at least 4 hours before serving.

Sweet Endings

In loving memory of my daddy,
James Williams, who had a serious Sweet Tooth!
His request at holidays was to always fix him
a cake plate to go. I love and miss you dearly.

Aunt Doris's Secret Candied Apples Recipe

MAKES 10 SERVINGS

- 2 Cups sugar
- 3/4 Cup light corn syrup
- 1/3 Cup water
- 1 Tbsp red food coloring
- 1 Tsp vanilla
- 10 Small apples

Add sugar, syrup and water. Bring to a boil on medium high heat. Cook for a few minutes. Add other ingredients. Cook on medium until thick. Test in cold water until crunchy. Cook about 10 minutes until it reaches 300° on a candy thermometer. This recipe will make about 10 candied apples.

Insert the candy apple stick into the apples. Dip the apples into the hot syrup to coat. Stand the apples up straight on buttered wax paper.

Aunt Doris would make the best candy apples, and even added toppings such as coconut and pecans. She rested them on buttered wax paper to give the top a delicious buttery flavor. She kept her candy apple recipe a secret for many years. I begged and begged for this recipe. One day, she finally gave it to me and said, "Don't you tell nobody!" So, I'm sharing Aunt Doris' secret recipe with you, but please, don't you tell nobody!

Bananas Foster Bread Pudding

MAKES 6-8 SERVINGS

- 1 Loaf of stale french or challah bread, broken into small pieces
- 1 Cup whole milk
- 4 Cups evaporated milk
- 2 1/2 Cups sugar
- 8 Tbsp butter, melted
- 4 Eggs
- 2 Tbsp vanilla extract
- 3 Bananas, sliced

Combine all ingredients. Pour into buttered 9 x 13 inch baking dish. Bake at 325° for 1 hour 15 minutes, checking to make sure it is not browning too fast.

Bananas Foster Sauce

Melt butter and add brown sugar. Stir until smooth. Stir in liquor (away from heat). Tilt pan or light pan with long lighter to catch sauce on fire. Let burn out, then add bananas and simmer for 2 minutes. Serve warm over bread pudding.

- 1/2 Cup butter
- 2 Cups brown sugar
- 4 Oz 151 rum
- 2 Oz banana liquor
- 2 Bananas, cut in small slices

Granddaddy Hastings worked at Winn Dixie warehouse in the bakery department. He would always bring home loaves and loaves of bread, so Grandma made bread pudding almost every week. Basically, what she put in it was – whatever she had available in the house at the time – raisins or pineapple or coconut – whatever. I was able to develop a recipe based on what she said and what I tasted. Grandma's bread pudding was always buttery good with crispy edges.

Butterscotch Pecan Pie

MAKES 6-8 SERVINGS

- 3 Eggs
- 1 Cup light corn syrup
- 1/2 Tsp salt
- 1 Tsp vanilla
- 2 Tbsp butterscotch liquor (optional)
- 1 Cup light brown sugar
- 2 Tbsp butter, melted
- 1 1/2 Cup pecan halves
- 9 Inch unbaked deep dish pie shell

Preheat oven to 400°. In medium bowl, beat eggs. Add corn syrup, salt, vanilla, butterscotch, brown sugar and butter. Mix well. Stir in nuts, pour into unbaked pie shell and bake for 15 minutes.

Reduce heat to 350° and bake an additional 30 to 35 minutes or until outer edge of filling seems set. Let cool completely.

Buttery Pie Crust

MAKES 2
9 INCH PIE CRUSTS

- 2 Cups flour
- 1/4 Tsp salt
- 2/3 Cup butter, cold
- 4-5 Tbsp cold water

Combine flour and salt in large bowl, cut in butter with a pastry cutter or fork until mixture resembles coarse crumbs. Stir in enough water with forks just until flour is moistened. Divide dough into two balls and refrigerate in plastic wrap.

Roll out 1 ball into 12 inch circle. Fold into quarters and place into a 9 inch pie pan; unfold dough, pressing firmly against bottom and sides. Trim crust to 1/2 inch from edge of pan. Crimp the edges.

Peanut Brittle

MAKES 1 1/4 POUNDS

- 2 Cups sugar
- 1 Cup light corn syrup
- 1 Cup water
- 2 Cups raw peanuts
- 1/4 Tsp salt
- 1 Tbsp butter
- 1/4 Tsp baking soda
- 1/2 Tsp vanilla extract
- Candy thermometer

Combine sugar, corn syrup and water in heavy saucepan. Cook slowly on medium heat, stirring constantly until the sugar dissolves.

Cook to soft ball stage as indicated on your candy thermometer (235°). Add peanuts and salt; cook beyond soft crack stage (290° to 300°). Add butter, soda and vanilla. Stir to blend (mixture will foam).

Pour onto 2 large, buttered cookie sheets. Spread lightly with a fork. Let it cool completely and then break into pieces.

Classic Peanut Butter Cookies

MAKES 2 DOZEN

- 1/2 Cup butter
- 1/2 Cup peanut butter
- 1/2 Cup sugar
- 1/2 Cup brown sugar
- 1 Egg
- 1/2 Tsp vanilla
- 1 1/4 Cup sifted flour
- 3/4 Tsp baking soda
- 1/4 Tsp salt

Preheat oven to 350°. Mix first six ingredients. Add the rest of the ingredients. Mix well. Roll into balls and press down with a fork dipped in sugar.

Bake for 10 minutes on an ungreased cookie sheet. Check at 7 minutes to make sure they are not cooking too fast. Remove from oven. Cool and enjoy.

Coconut Cake

MAKES 12-14 SERVINGS

- 1 Stick vegetable shortening*
- 1 Stick of butter or margarine
- 2 Cups sugar
- 4 Eggs
- 3 Cups self-rising flour
- 1 Cup whole milk
- 1 Tsp vanilla extract
- 1/2 Cup shredded coconut

Preheat oven to 350°. Grease and flour 2 – 9 inch pans.

In a large bowl, cream together shortening, butter and sugar until light and fluffy. Add eggs, 1 at a time, mixing in between. Mix in flour and milk, alternately, using half at a time. Mix in vanilla and coconut. Pour batter into prepared pans.

Bake 30 minutes in preheated oven until center springs back when lightly touched.

Icing

ICING:

- 1 – 8 Oz package cream cheese
- 1 Box 10x powdered sugar
- 1/2 Stick butter, melted
- 1 Tsp vanilla
- 1 Cup shredded coconut

Beat together all ingredients, except coconut, until smooth. Ice cake with cream cheese mixture and top with coconut.

Crème Brulee

MAKES 6 SERVINGS

- **1 Quart heavy cream**
- **1 Vanilla bean, split and scraped**
- **1/2 Cup sugar**
- **6 Egg yolks**
- **Hot water**
- **1/2 Cup unbleached sugar***

This is one of my favorite French Classical desserts. I love the crunchy topping with the creamy custard underneath. Any effort to jazz it up takes away from the simple goodness of this dish. Southern goodness equals simple goodness. Keep it simple. It is perfect just the way it is.

Preheat oven to 325°.

Place the cream and vanilla bean and seeds into a medium saucepan. Bring to a slow boil. Remove from heat and let sit for 10 minutes. Remove vanilla bean.

In a medium bowl, whisk together sugar and the egg yolks well, until the mixture starts to turn pale yellow. Add the cream to the egg mixture slowly, stirring constantly. Pour liquid into 6 – 8 ounce ramekins. Place the ramekins into a large roasting pan. Pour enough hot water into the roasting pan to come halfway up the sides of the ramekins.

Bake for 40 minutes or until crème brulee is set. Remove from roasting pan and refrigerate.

Remove the crème brulee from the refrigerator. Divide the unbleached sugar evenly between each ramekin, sprinkling on the top. Using a torch, melt the sugar to form a crispy top.

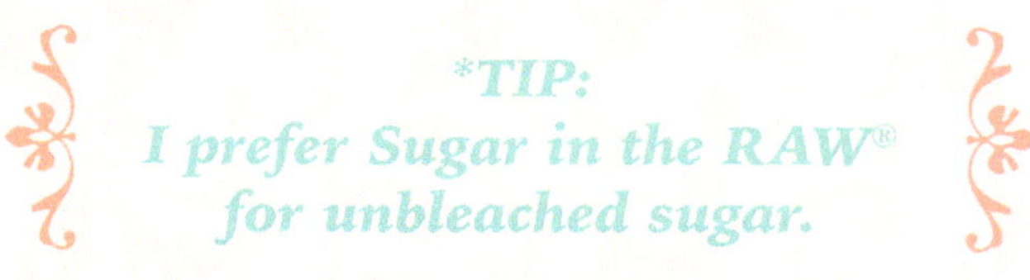

***TIP:**
I prefer Sugar in the RAW® for unbleached sugar.

Grand Marnier Chocolate Meringue Torte

MAKES 12-14 SERVINGS

MERINGUE:

- 6 Egg whites
- 1/2 Tsp salt
- 1/2 Tsp cream of tartar
- 1 Tbsp Grand Marnier liqueur
- 1 1/2 Cups sugar
- 2 Tbsp orange zest

FILLING:

- 6 Oz semisweet chocolate (chopped or chips)
- 1 Cup mini marshmallows
- 2/3 Cup evaporated milk
- 2 Tbsp Grand Marnier liqueur
- 1 Cup whipping cream

Preheat oven to 300°.

In a large mixing bowl, beat egg whites, salt, cream of tartar and Grand Marnier at high speed until soft peaks form. Gradually add sugar and orange zest, then beat until stiff peaks are formed. Spread meringue on greased and floured baking sheet, making 3 six inch circles.

Bake for 25 to 30 minutes until lightly browned. Remove from baking sheet immediately. Cool layers. Spread chocolate filling in between each layer and on top. Chill in the refrigerator 6 to 8 hours or overnight.

Chocolate Filling

In medium saucepan, heat chocolate, marshmallows, milk and Grand Marnier Liqueur stirring constantly until mixture is melted. Chill. Beat whipping cream until thick. Fold in chocolate mixture.

Granny's Old Fashioned Chocolate Icing

MAKES ENOUGH FOR A 3 LAYER CAKE

- **2 Cups sugar**
- **1 Stick of butter or margarine**
- **2 1/2 Tbsp chocolate**
- **1 Tsp vanilla**
- **1 – 5 Oz can evaporated milk**

Bring all ingredients to a boil. Cook 5 minutes on medium heat, stirring constantly.

NOTE: The cake recipe for this can be made the same way as the coconut cake on page 156 – minus the coconut.

This is my absolute favorite, favorite, favorite of all things. I double this recipe because I like to have tons of icing just running on the plate. Granny made it for every holiday, along with many other desserts, however, this is the one that I would run to first. The cake is important, but this icing will make any cake delicious! It was also my Aunt Dedra's favorite.

Hummingbird Cake

MAKES 8-10 SERVINGS

- 3 Cups flour
- 2 Cups sugar
- 1 Tsp baking soda
- 1 Tsp salt
- 1 Tsp ground cinnamon
- 3 Eggs, beaten
- 1 Cup vegetable oil
- 1 1/2 Tsp vanilla
- 8 Oz can crushed pineapple
- 1 Cup chopped pecans
- 1 Cup smashed bananas

ICING:

- 1 – 8 Oz package cream cheese
- 1 Box 10x powdered sugar
- 1/2 Stick butter, melted
- 1 Tsp vanilla
- 1 Cup pecans

Combine first five ingredients. Add eggs and oil. Stir until moistened. Stir in vanilla, pineapple, pecans, and bananas. Spoon batter into 3 greased and floured 9 inch pans.

Bake at 350° for 20 to 25 minutes. Cool completely before removing from pans.

Icing

Beat together all ingredients until smooth, except pecans. Add pecans and combine by stirring with spoon.

A very dear friend of mine, the late Angela Chestnut, use to make this cake on special occasions for many of our mutual friends. I later discovered that it is very common in many Southern cookbooks – a classic Southern dessert. But, like a fingerprint, every recipe has the unique signature of the cook. When you make this recipe, make it your own!

Italian Cream Cake

MAKES 8-10 SERVINGS

- 2 Cups sugar
- 5 Eggs, separated
- 1 Stick of butter
- 1/2 Cup shortening
- 1 Tsp baking soda
- 1 Cup buttermilk
- 2 Cups sifted flour
- 1 Tsp vanilla
- 2 Cups coconut
- 1 Cup chopped pecans

FROSTING:

- 1/2 Stick butter
- 1 – 8 Oz package of cream cheese
- 1 Box powdered sugar
- 1 Tsp vanilla
- 1 Cup chopped pecans

Cream sugar and egg yolks and add 1 stick butter and shortening; beat well. Combine soda with buttermilk and add alternately with flour. Add vanilla, coconut, and pecans. Fold in stiffly beaten egg whites. If making 3 layers, bake 30 minutes on 350°. If making bundt pan, bake for 1 hour. Grease and flour pans and frost cake when cooled.

Frosting

Cream butter and cream cheese, beat in powdered sugar and add vanilla, add nuts. Stir until well blended.

**TIP:*
I prefer Crisco® Shortening.

Key Lime Cake

MAKES 8-10 SERVINGS

- 1 Package lemon cake mix
- 1 – 3 Oz package lime gelatin mix
- 1 1/3 Cups vegetable oil
- 4 Eggs
- 3/4 Cup orange juice

FROSTING:

- 1/2 Cup butter
- 1 – 8 Oz package of cream cheese
- 3 Tbsp fresh lime juice
- 4 Cups powdered sugar

Heat oven to 325°. Grease and flour 3 – 8 inch cake pans.

Combine cake mix, gelatin mix, oil, eggs and orange juice. Pour into 3 – 8 inch cake pans. Bake for 25 minutes or until toothpick comes out clean. Allow to cool, then frost.

Key Lime Cake Frosting

In a large bowl, beat the butter and cream cheese until light and fluffy. Add lime juice and powdered sugar. Mix well.

Lemon Meringue Pie

MAKES 6-8 SERVINGS

PIE CRUST:

- 1 1/3 Cups all purpose flour
- 1/2 Tsp salt
- 4 Tbsp cold unsalted butter, thinly sliced
- 4 Tbsp cold lard
- 3 Tbsp ice water

FILLING:

- 1 1/2 Cup sugar
- 6 Tbsp cornstarch
- 1/4 Tsp salt
- 3 Egg yolks, well beaten
- 1/2 Cup fresh lemon juice
- 1/2 Cup cold water
- 1 Tsp lemon zest
- 2 Tbsp butter

MERINGUE:

- 4 Egg whites
- 1/4 Tsp salt
- 1/2 Cup sugar

PIE CRUST: In large bowl, combine flour and salt. Using a pastry cutter cut the butter and lard into the flour until the mixture resembles coarse meal. Add the ice water as you toss the mixture with a fork. Gather the dough together into a ball and knead it 2 or 3 times, until evenly moistened. Pat the dough into a 6 inch disk, wrap the pastry in plastic and chill in refrigerator for at least 1 hour.

Preheat oven to 375°. On a lightly floured surface, roll out the chilled dough to 12 inches round, 1/8 inch thick. Fit the dough into a 9 inch pie plate and trim the overhang to 1/2 inch. Fold the overhang under and crimp it decoratively. Line the uncooked dough with foil and fill with pie weights or dried beans. Set the pie shell on a baking sheet and bake for 15 minutes, or until the edge is set. Carefully remove the foil and weights and bake the shell for 15 minutes longer, or until the bottom is firm and light golden. If the crust begins to brown too quickly, loosely cover the edge with foil. Transfer to a wire rack to cool.

FILLING: In a medium saucepan, combine sugar with cornstarch, salt, egg yolks and lemon juice. Whisk in the cold water and cook the mixture over moderate heat, whisking constantly for 1 minute. Remove the mixture from the heat and add the lemon zest and butter, stirring until the butter is melted. Pour the lemon curd filling into the baked crust. Cover with plastic wrap and let cool at room temperature.

MERINGUE: Preheat oven to 350°. Position rack in the upper third of the oven. In a large stainless steel bowl, beat the egg whites with the salt at high speed until soft peaks form. Gradually add sugar and beat the egg whites until they are stiff and glossy peaks have formed.

Using the back of a spoon, spread the meringue onto the pie making decorative swirls in the meringue. Bake for about 7 minutes or until meringue is golden brown. Let cool at room temperature. Refrigerate for about 3 hours.

Oatmeal Cookies

MAKES 4 DOZEN

- 1 Cup butter or margarine
- 1 Cup brown sugar, firmly packed
- 1/2 Cup sugar
- 2 Eggs
- 1 Tsp vanilla
- 1 1/2 Cup all purpose flour
- 1 Tsp baking soda
- 1 Tsp cinnamon
- 1/2 Tsp salt
- 3 Cups oatmeal, uncooked
- 1/2 Cup raisins
- 1/2 Cup walnuts

Heat oven to 350°.

Beat together butter and sugars until creamy. Add eggs and vanilla; beat well.

Combine flour, baking soda, cinnamon and salt. Add to butter/sugar mixture. Stir well.

Stir in oats, raisins and walnuts. Mix well. Drop by rounded tablespoonful's onto ungreased cookie sheet.

Bake 10 to 12 minutes or until golden brown.

No Bake Oatmeal Peanut Butter Cookies

MAKES 15 COOKIES

- 2 Cups sugar
- 4 Tbsp cocoa
- 1 Stick of butter
- 1/2 Cup whole milk
- 1 Cup peanut butter
- 1 Tsp vanilla
- 3 Cups quick oatmeal unflavored*

Bring sugar, cocoa, butter and milk to a boil. Let boil 1 minute. Add peanut butter, vanilla and oatmeal. Drop by rounded tablespoonful's onto wax paper. Let cool.

TIP:
This oatmeal is not the steel cut hearty oatmeal, but rather the quick oatmeal that can be found in your grocer isle.

Old-Fashioned Jelly Cake

MAKES 12-14 SERVINGS

- 1 Stick shortening
- 1 Stick or butter or margarine
- 2 Cups sugar
- 4 Eggs
- 3 Cups self-rising flour
- 1 Cup whole milk
- 1 Tsp vanilla extract
- 2 Cups apple jelly
- 3 Tbsp of butter, melted

Preheat oven to 350°. Grease and flour 2 – 9 inch pans.

In a large bowl, cream together butter, sugar and shortening until light and fluffy. Add eggs, 1 at a time, mixing in between. Mix in flour and milk, alternately, using half at a time. Mix in vanilla. Pour batter into prepared pans.

Bake 30 minutes in preheated oven until center springs back when lightly touched.

Mix together apple jelly and melted butter with a fork, while cake is baking.

Poke holes in warm cake layers and spread jelly over cake while cake is warm so that jelly will soak into cake. Top with the remaining cake layer, spread jelly on top and sides.

**TIP:*
I prefer Crisco® Shortening.

This was not one of my favorite cakes growing up, because I loved my Granny's chocolate cake. But, it was always on the table. It was only when my mother-in-law kept asking about it that I decided to make it. That's when I discovered that it was really good, and learned that it really is another Southern tradition and not just one of Granny's cakes.

Pea Picking Cake

MAKES 8-10 SERVINGS

- **1 Box yellow cake mix**
- **1 1/2 Cup vegetable oil**
- **4 Eggs**
- **1 Small can mandarin oranges (juice and all)**

Prep 3 round cake pans, grease and flour them. Mix all ingredients together well. Bake at 350° for 30 minutes. Let cool before icing.

Icing

ICING:

- **1 Large can crushed pineapple, with juice**
- **1 Package 3.7 box of instant vanilla pudding**
- **1 Large container frozen whipped topping.**

Mix pineapple and juice with vanilla pudding. Mix with frozen whipped topping. Mix well and spread on layers of cake and chill.

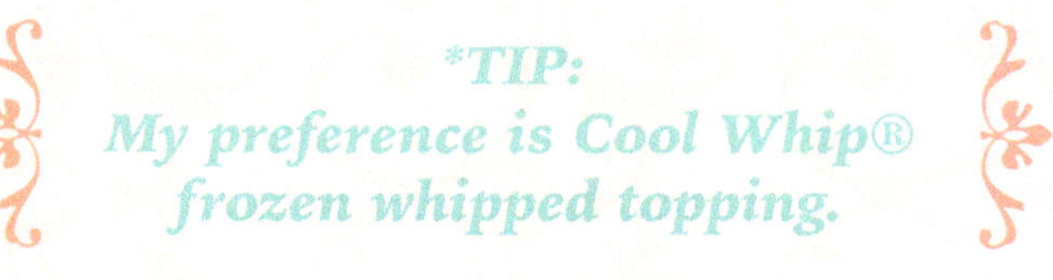

Cream Cheese Pound Cake

MAKES 8-10 SERVINGS

- 3 Sticks butter
- 1 – 8 Oz package cream cheese
- 3 Cups sugar
- 6 Eggs, med. (5 large)
- 1 Tsp vanilla extract
- 1/2 Tsp lemon extract
- 3 Cups cake flour or all-purpose flour
- Dash of salt

Cream together butter, cream cheese, and sugar very well. Add eggs one at a time. Beat after each egg is added. Add extracts. Sift salt and flour together. Add flour and mix until well combined.

Put in a bundt cake pan and cook for 1 hour and 15 minutes at 325° and check at the hour mark with a tooth pick and see if it comes out clean.

Peanut Butter Cup Mini Muffins

MAKES 30 SERVINGS

- 1/2 Cup butter
- 1/2 Cup peanut butter
- 1/2 Cup sugar
- 1/2 Cup brown sugar
- 1 Egg
- 1/2 Tsp vanilla
- 1 1/4 Cup sifted flour
- 3/4 Tsp baking soda
- 1/4 Tsp salt
- 30 Miniature peanut butter cups, unwrapped

Preheat oven to 375°. Mix first six ingredients. Add the rest of the ingredients. Mix well. Shape cookie dough into 1/2 inch balls and place balls into an ungreased mini muffin pan.

Bake at 375° for about 8 minutes. Remove from oven and immediately press a mini peanut butter cup into each muffin. Cool and carefully remove from pan.

I love peanut butter cookies! I love peanut butter cups! For over 20 years now, I have been combining my love for peanut butter cookies and peanut butter cups into my very-often requested peanut butter cup mini muffins. My family and clients love these tremendously, Reese's® should be paying me for promoting their peanut butter cups!

Pecan Rum Cake

MAKES 12-14 SERVINGS

- 1 Cup pecans, chopped
- 1 – 18.25 Oz yellow cake mix
- 1 – 3.4 Oz package instant vanilla pudding
- 4 Eggs
- 1/2 Cup water
- 1/2 Cup vegetable oil
- 1/2 Cup dark rum

GLAZE:

- 1/2 Cup butter
- 1/4 Cup water
- 1 Cup sugar
- 1/2 Cup dark rum

Preheat oven to 325°. Grease and flour a bundt pan. Add pecans to the bottom of the cake pan.

In a large bowl, combine cake mix and pudding mix. Mix in the eggs, 1/2 cup water, oil and 1/2 cup rum. Blend well. Pour batter over chopped nuts in the pan.

Bake for 60 minutes, or until a toothpick inserted into the cake comes out clean.

While the cake is baking, make the glaze: In a saucepan, combine butter, 1/4 cup water and 1 cup sugar. Bring to a boil over medium heat and boil for 5 minutes, stirring constantly. Remove from heat and stir in 1/2 cup rum.

Poke holes in cake with a skewer and brush glaze over top and sides, until cake absorbs all of the glaze.

Pecan Pralines

MAKES 30 SERVINGS

- 1 Cup light brown sugar
- 1/2 Cup sugar
- 1/2 Cup heavy cream
- 4 Tbsp butter
- 2 Tbsp water
- 1 Cup pecans

Combine brown sugar, sugar, heavy cream, butter and water in a heavy sauce pot. Cook over medium heat, stirring constantly until mixture reaches 240°. Remove from heat and stir in pecans. Stir for an additional 2 minutes.

Spoon pralines on parchment paper greased with butter. Allow to cool before serving.

Pecan Turtle Candies

MAKES 25 CANDIES

- 1 Lb pecan halves, toasted
- 1 – 14 Oz Can evaporated milk
- 3/4 Cup light corn syrup
- 1/2 Cup sugar
- 1/3 Cup packed light brown sugar
- 1/4 Cup butter, cubed
- 1 1/2 Tsp vanilla extract
- 1 Lb milk chocolate candy coating

On waxed paper-lined baking sheets, arrange pecans in small clusters.

CARAMEL: In a small saucepan, combine milk, corn syrup, brown sugar and sugar. Stir over medium heat until candy thermometer reads 238° (soft ball stage). Remove from heat. Stir in butter and vanilla. Quickly spoon on top of pecans.

Melt chocolate in microwave in 30 second increments, stirring well. Spoon over caramel. Chill until chocolate is set. Store in an airtight container.

Raspberry Thumbprint Cookies

MAKES 24 COOKIES

- 1 3/4 Cups all-purpose flour
- 1/2 Tsp baking powder
- 1 1/2 Sticks butter
- 2/3 Cup sugar
- 1 Large egg
- 1 Tsp vanilla extract
- 1/3 Cup raspberry jam

Preheat oven to 350°. Line baking sheet pan with parchment paper.

Whisk together flour and baking powder in a bowl.

In another bowl, combine butter and sugar and beat until fluffy. Beat in egg and vanilla until just combined. Slowly add in dry ingredients. Beat to combine.

Scoop out dough into 1 inch balls with cookie scoop. Place 2 inches apart on baking sheets. Place a thumbprint into the center of each ball and fill indentation with raspberry jam.

Bake cookies for 15 minutes or until edges are golden brown.

Red Velvet Cake

MAKES 8-10 SERVINGS

- 1 1/2 Cup sugar
- 2 Cups vegetable oil
- 3 Eggs
- 1 Tbsp white vinegar
- 2 Oz red food coloring
- 2 1/2 Cup cake flour
- 1 Tsp baking soda
- 1 Tsp salt
- 1 1/2 Tbsp cocoa
- 1 Cup buttermilk
- 1 Tsp vanilla

ICING:

- 1 – 8 Oz package cream cheese
- 1 Box 10x powdered sugar
- 1/2 Stick butter, melted
- 1 Tsp vanilla
- 1 Cup pecans

Preheat oven to 350°. Grease and flour 3 – 8 inch round cake pans.

Cream sugar and oil; add eggs and beat well. Add vinegar and food coloring to mix. Sift all dry ingredients. Add dry ingredients, buttermilk and vanilla. Mix well. Pour evenly into 3 prepared cake pans. Bake at 350° for 30 to 35 minutes.

Icing

Beat together all ingredients until smooth, except pecans. Add pecans and combine by stirring with spoon.

People think the Red Velvet Cake is really complicated, but it's not. It is actually very simple. This is another one of my Aunt Doris's favorite recipes, as well as one of the most requested desserts from clients.

Shortbread Cookies

MAKES 5 DOZEN

- 2 Cups all purpose flour
- 1 Cup powdered sugar
- 1/4 Tsp baking soda
- 1 Cup unsalted butter, melted

Mix flour, sugar, and baking soda together. Add melted butter. Mix together. Bake on 350 for 10 minutes or until edges are light brown.

Salted Caramel Sauce

MAKES 4 SERVINGS

- 1 Cup sugar
- 1/4 Cup water
- 3/4 Cup heavy cream
- 4 Tbsp butter
- 1 Tsp kosher salt

In a heavy-bottomed saucepan, combine the sugar and water over medium-low heat until the sugar dissolves. Increase heat and bring to a boil, without stirring. Boil until the mixture turns to an amber color, about 5 minutes.

Remove mixture from heat and slowly whisk in heavy cream, being careful because mixture will bubble up. Stir in butter and salt. Transfer from pan to cool.

There are fancy, decadent indulgences; then, there are very simple ones. This is as simple as it gets, but it is just as decadent! There's just something about mixing salty and sweet. Whether drizzled on top of ice cream or brownies, or just a few spoons full by itself, this simple goodness is worth every calorie.

Rice Pudding

MAKES 6-8 SERVINGS

- 4 Cups whole milk, divided
- 1/2 Cup rice
- 1/2 Cup sugar, divided
- 1 Egg
- Dash of nutmeg
- 1 Tsp vanilla
- Cinnamon

Mix in bowl slowly 3 cups milk, rice, and 1/4 cup sugar. Add to a medium heavy bottom pot and cook on medium heat until rice is cooked; stir constantly.

Beat egg and remaining sugar until creamy. Add 1 cup milk and beat well. Add nutmeg and vanilla. Add to cooked rice mixture. Let boil slowly for 5 minutes. Pour into glass casserole and sprinkle with cinnamon. Chill.

Glazed Pecans

MAKES 4-6 SERVINGS

- 2 Tbsp butter
- 2 Tbsp dark brown sugar
- 2 Tbsp maple syrup
- 2 Cups pecans
- 1/4 Tsp vanilla extract

Heat oven to 350°.

Line cookie sheet with parchment paper. In skillet, melt butter. Add brown sugar and syrup; mix well. Cook until bubbly, stirring constantly. Add pecans and vanilla extract. Cook 2 to 3 minutes, stirring constantly, until coated. Spread mixture onto parchment paper lined cookie sheet.

Bake for 6 to 8 minutes or until golden brown. Let cool completely, about 30 minutes.

Sweet Potato Pie

MAKES 6-8 SERVINGS

- 1 Lb sweet potatoes, ends cut off
- 2 Large eggs
- 1 Stick of butter
- 1 Cup sugar
- 1/2 Tsp nutmeg
- 1 Tsp vanilla extract
- 1/4 Cup evaporated milk
- 9 Inch deep dish unbaked pie shell

Preheat oven to 325

In a large pot add potatoes, cover with water and boil uncovered until fork tender (about 30 minutes). Drain well. Run cold water on potatoes to cool and peel.

Add eggs, butter, sugar, nutmeg, vanilla and milk. Beat until smooth with mixer. Take mixer beaters off and rinse strings away. Mix again with beaters. Pour mixture into pie crust and bake 35 to 45 minutes until golden.

Index

S

T

V

Z

About the Author

Executive Chef Celestia Mobley has the most successful soul food restaurant in Jacksonville, Florida. Celeste (as she is affectionately known) shares the secrets of her paternal grandmother's favorite dishes at The Potter's House Soul Food Bistro. She began cooking at the tender age of 8, watching her grandmother prepare family dinners with love every Sunday and for holiday gatherings.

Deciding not to continue with her 10 year career in banking, she opened her first seafood restaurant to follow her dream. After completing her degree in Culinary Management, she traveled throughout Europe on a culinary tour polishing her skills. Upon returning, her pastor, Bishop McLaughlin, expressed a desire to expand his church's food ministry. He spoke to Celeste about managing the new Potter's House Restaurants.

In addition to being the Executive Chef and General Manager of The Potter's House Soul Food Bistro, Celeste also serves on the board of The American Culinary Federation, through which she participates in the Chef and Child Program.

About the Book

The heart of *Southern Goodness* is about food and family; treasuring the family meals from your childhood, remembering special Sunday dinners and Family cookouts.

For Executive Chef Celestia Mobley, those family gatherings were a magical time to truly enjoy each others company and keep up with family traditions.

In her debut cookbook, *Southern Goodness,* Chef Mobley will make you feel right at home as she makes her Granny's famous fried chicken—moist and tender on the inside; and crispy on the outside...along with many other amazing dishes sure to remind you of family and home.

Cooking with love is easier than you think. *Southern Goodness* has simple recipes that are not complicated or elaborate. Every meal is special when you follow Chef Mobley's motto of, "Cook with love, live with passion, and laugh often!" Come join us for some *Southern Goodness* where Celestia's recipes will tickle your taste buds and warm your heart. We'll leave a seat at the table for you!

www.ingramcontent.com/pod-product-compliance
Lightning Source LLC
Chambersburg PA
CBHW040300100426
42811CB00011B/1321

* 9 7 8 0 9 9 6 3 6 7 1 0 3 *